The Book of
Ho'oponopono

"Ho'oponopono is an important practice of compassion, forgiveness, and gratitude, both for our relationships and for ourselves. Drawing on its rich history, Bodin, Lamboy, and Graciet explore—with depth and insight—the many layers of this powerful tool for mediation and healing. Their book gives us a compelling approach to cultivating this practice in our everyday lives."

BAIRD HERSEY, MUSICIAN AND AUTHOR OF
THE PRACTICE OF NADA YOGA

"Nowhere has the Hawaiian healing practice of Ho'oponopono been explored as extensively as within this book. The authors give us a thorough guide to humble our way of life to accord with the way things truly are, through the life practice of forgiveness that ultimately leads to the peace and love we all deeply yearn for. Drawing not only from this ancient Hawaiian tradition but also from modern science, this book gives us the tools to live a more authentic life through facing our accumulated karma that obstructs our innate freedom."

JASON GREGORY, AUTHOR OF *ENLIGHTENMENT NOW*
AND *THE SCIENCE AND PRACTICE OF HUMILITY*

"Blessed are the ones who free future generations of irrational fear. The inherent power of forgiveness can mean our very survival. *The Book of Ho'oponopono* tells you how to be free of the ropes of fear and grief and attachment to old and unworkable ways. In this book, learn and marvel at the impact on relationships and mental health by saying to yourself, 'I'm sorry, forgive me, thank you, I love you.' The authors, each in their own specialties, ground the mystical with science and guide the reader in the gentle Hawaiian way of soft breezes and blue surf to increasingly take charge of the past, past lives, and even unknown issues—to be free of memories and beliefs that can be like storm clouds hiding us from our true island self."

GARNETTE ARLEDGE, COAUTHOR OF
WISE SECRETS OF ALOHA:
LEARN AND LIVE THE SACRED ART OF LOMILOMI

The Book of
Ho'oponopono

The Hawaiian Practice of
Forgiveness and Healing

Luc Bodin, M.D.,
Nathalie Bodin Lamboy,
and Jean Graciet

Translated by Jon E. Graham

Destiny Books
Rochester, Vermont • Toronto, Canada

Destiny Books
One Park Street
Rochester, Vermont 05767
www.DestinyBooks.com

Destiny Books is a division of Inner Traditions International

Originally published in French under the title *Le grand livre de Ho'oponopono: Sagesse hawaïenne de guérison* by Éditions Jouvence, www.editions-jouvence.com, info@editions-jouvence.com
First U.S. edition published in 2016 by Destiny Books

Library of Congress Cataloging-in-Publication Data

Bodin, Luc, 1954–
 [Grand livre de ho'oponopono. English]
 The book of ho'oponopono : the Hawaiian practice of forgiveness and healing / Luc Bodin, Nathalie Bodin Lamboy, Jean Graciet.
  pages cm
 Includes bibliographical references and index.
 ISBN 978-1-62055-510-1 (pbk) — ISBN 978-1-62055-511-8 (e-book)
 1. Mental healing. 2. Forgiveness. 3. Mind and body therapies. 4. Mind and body—Religious aspects. 5. Alternative medicine—Hawaii. 6. Spiritual life. I. Title.
 RZ401.B66713 2016
 615.8'528—dc23

                                                                    2015029192

Printed and bound in China by Reliance Printing Co., Ltd.

10 9 8

Text design and layout by Priscilla Baker
This book was typeset in Garamond Premier Pro with Cantoria and Gill Sans used as display typefaces
Illustrations by Jean Augagneur
To send correspondence to the authors of this book, mail a first-class letter to the authors c/o Inner Traditions • Bear & Company, One Park Street, Rochester, VT 05767, and we will forward the communication, or contact the authors directly at **www.luc-bodin.us, www.livinghooponopono.com,** or **www.mercijetaime.fr.**

Contents

Foreword

When my friend Luc asked me to write the foreword for this book, that very evening I pulled a book at random from the shelf of my home library and opened it absentmindedly. Inside I found a piece of paper folded in half on which I had written these sentences:

> In my opinion, there must be something behind all this . . . a completely simple notion. And this notion for me, when we finally discover it, will be so irresistible and fine that we will say to ourselves, "Oh, how could it have been anything else!" (John Wheeler, physicist, quote from a 1985 television documentary, *The Creation of the Universe*)

The silence whispered to me that these sentences were a wink of the eye from life to remind me of what is essential.

This is the way truths make their way to us. Always simple, they do not offer explanations and need no long speeches.

This is how Ho'oponopono came into my life. My heart recognized something it already knew, because our hearts are designed to recognize the truth.

The problem is that we have a kind of veil that prevents us from seeing and expressing our true nature. In Ho'oponopono this veil is made of memories. In order to clarify and dissolve them, we all have one simple thing we must do: cleanse, cleanse, cleanse.

Over time I realized that this "cleansing" takes place in three stages. First, we must open our hearts; then, we welcome "what is" with love. Finally, we have to learn to let go of the veil, stop clinging, and trust in the God we all carry within ourselves.

In this book my friends Nathalie Bodin Lamboy and Luc Bodin, and my husband, Jean, share their experience and knowledge of Ho'oponopono, thereby giving you the opportunity to advance your understanding of this way of being in the world.

Through practice you will be able to discover and integrate the path that is most appropriate for you, the one that speaks to you from your heart.

Open your heart and remember: "It is only with the heart that one can see clearly; what is essential is invisible to the eye" (Antoine de Saint-Exupéry, *The Little Prince*).

I am grateful for the opportunity life has given me to clear this veil that keeps me in the illusion of separation.

I speak to the unique being that I am, to Mother Earth, and to you, the reader, knowing that my first mistake is in believing I am separate from the All and imperfect. I ask my soul, or my higher self, to help me release all the memories that make me believe this.

I'm sorry, forgive me, thank you, I love you.

MARIE-ELISA HURTADO-GRACIET

Marie-Elisa Hurtado-Graciet gives lectures and workshops on Ho'oponopono and EFT (Emotional Freedom Technique) in France and abroad. She is also an NLP (Neuro-Linguistic Programming) practitioner and the author of several books, including *Ho'oponopono: Le secret des guérisseurs hawaïens.*

Operating Instructions for Ho'oponopono

The Ho'oponopono phrase:
"I'm sorry, forgive me, thank you, I love you."

What do these words mean?
"I'm sorry" is acknowledgment that I created whatever pain I've caused or errors I've made.

"Forgive me," because I did not know I had that inside me.

"Thank you" for allowing me to release and cleanse this memory.

"I love you," my inner divinity, meaning, "I love me."

When should this phrase be said?
When you are confronted by a conflict, a violent reaction, an accident, a traumatic event, anything that causes a strong, negative emotion to surge up within you.

How should it be said?
You can say it out loud or quietly to yourself.

To whom are you speaking when you say this phrase?
To yourself, your inner divinity, your protectors, the universe, God.

Can this phrase be used preventively?
You can say, "I'm sorry, forgive me, thank you, I love you," even when you are not experiencing any actual conflict. This allows you to erase any memories that have emerged without your knowledge. Some people recite this phrase as a mantra when they are taking a walk, hiking, or riding a bike.

Can you say this phrase during a happy event?
Yes, you have at your disposal a tool that allows you to put your ego to bed and fully experience joy, in complete humility.

Can you do Ho'oponopono while watching television?
You can perform Ho'oponopono in the context of anything that inspires negative emotion, including television, the Internet, telephone, or listening to the radio.

Must you say every word of the phrase?
When you begin practicing Ho'oponopono, take the time to speak the full phrase until you have fully integrated the sensation of each word. After this, "Thank you, I love you" is enough.

What happens after you say it?
A sense of calm is established. You have no expectations about what is happening because the essential benefit of Ho'oponopono is that you achieve inner peace.

From the Origins of the Practice to Today

Jean Graciet

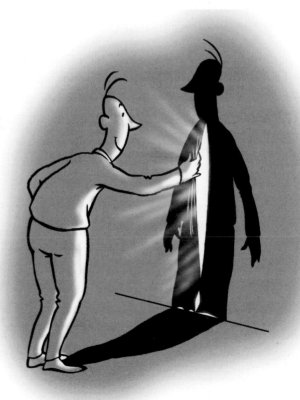

Beginning the Ho'oponopono process is relatively simple, when all is said and done. If something is bothering you, either a small daily annoyance or some much more serious event, all you need to do is repeat its four short phrases, which, in fact, are only a few words. These phrases are: "I'm sorry, forgive me, thank you, I love you." When these phrases are repeated several times over a certain interval, something happens—sometimes even a miracle takes place. Indeed, nothing could seem simpler, and it appears to be in the reach of everyone. But what we are going to see now is that it is not as simple as it looks to practice Ho'oponopono and integrate it into your life.

History of Ho'oponopono

Ho'oponopono is an essential element of Huna, the traditional healing and spiritual shamanism of Hawaii. Formerly a carefully guarded secret, the process is now available for all to use in creating harmony in their lives and peace in the world. It is both a philosophy and a state of mind, and embracing this process requires us to integrate ideas that are quite different from the ones we are accustomed to in Judeo-Christian traditions. Ho'oponopono leads us to look at others and ourselves in a way that is entirely different, if not diametrically opposite. This is where the practice of Ho'oponopono becomes much more complex and demands a significant shift in many people's beliefs and values.

Ho'oponopono is an ancestral Hawaiian custom that traditionally was invoked "to make right, establish harmony, correct what is wrong, and restore things to order." When individuals had disagreements, or relational problems appeared in a com-

munity, everyone gathered in the presence of all the protago-
nists and there, under the guidance of a *kahuna* (priest), all
were granted forgiveness.

 Ho‘oponopono is a process of atonement or reconciliation among individuals of the same family or
community.

Morrnah Simeona

This was the custom when shaman and plant healer Morrnah
Simeona began to develop a new form of the practice in 1976.
Morrnah had been born into a family of healers. Her mother
was a *kahuna lapa‘au kahea* (one who heals with words and
chants) who served Queen Lili‘uokalani, the last monarch and
only female ruler of the Kingdom of Hawaii, as lady-in-waiting.
The young protégée began her oral training in this living tradition at age three, and she practiced the healing arts throughout
her life, also becoming a master in Lomi Lomi healing massage.

Morrnah maintained that the process of Ho‘oponopono
could be greatly simplified by eliminating the presence of a guide
or priest, and that all individuals could practice it by themselves.
The way she taught Ho‘oponopono and introduced it at the
Huna World Convention in 1980 is the process we know today.
Using her approach, individuals can personally grant themselves
forgiveness, love, and peace on their own. This fact is important because it shows the extent to which the process has been
adapted to contemporary times, in which every individual is
guided to increasingly take charge of him- or herself.

Morrnah also said that we are weighed down by our memories. The objective of Ho‘oponopono is, therefore, to free
ourselves of these memories and beliefs so that, by getting rid

of the veil they form, we can discover the divinity within each one of us. In this way it will be possible to discover who we really are, which is an essential step.

With this process, and guided by the divinity within, memories are freed and transmuted into pure energy. This could be described as a kind of alchemical process in which fears and memories are transmuted into pure love.

For Morrnah Simeona, who was named a Living Treasure of Hawaii, "Peace starts with me and no one else."

Dr. Ihaleakala Hew Len

Dr. Ihaleakala Hew Len became Morrnah Simeona's best-known student, for it was through his efforts and extraordinary testimony that Ho'oponopono spread across the globe.

Dr. Len's story has made its way around the world, and all those who have been introduced to Ho'oponopono know it to some extent. A clinical psychologist, he was asked to head a ward for the criminally insane at the Hawaii State Hospital. It should be stressed that the atmosphere was heavy and odious, and danger was such a daily threat that staffers were in a constant state of fear. Absenteeism was high and staff psychologists did not remain there long.

Despite all this, Dr. Len accepted the position. He asked to see the patients' case files when he started the job, and then shut himself up alone in his office each day, insisting that no one disturb him. It was strange for a psychologist not to see the patients, but his wishes were respected.

Time passed and after a period of around three months, it was noted that the ambiance of the facility and relations with the patients had gradually improved. The staff pointed this out to the doctor and questioned him as to what he had been doing alone in his office, for his attitude continued to be a source of puzzlement.

Dr. Len then explained that he had cleansed the memories he had in common with each patient when he was studying each one's case file.

They asked, "How did you do it?"

He answered that he had simply repeated, "I'm sorry, forgive me, I thank you, I love you."

The staff was incredulous and asked, "And that's all?"

"That's all."

 Dr. Len explained that he had cleansed the memories he had in common with each patient simply by repeating, "I'm sorry, forgive me, I thank you, I love you."

He continued in this way at his post for close to four years, and at the end of this time, the psychiatric ward closed its doors, for there were no more patients. Either they had been cured or it was no longer necessary for them to remain in that ward.

How Did This Happen?

When talking about all these people he had cured, Dr. Len explained that he had healed the part of himself that had created them. He added that everything in our lives, everything that happens to us, is our responsibility. This means that everything we perceive with our five senses—the world surrounding us—is our creation. Consequently, Dr. Len perceived that it was his responsibility to heal the memories within himself that had created this particular situation.

Physical Reality Is a Creation of Your Thoughts

What exists outside of you is, in fact, only a projection of something that comes from you, something that could be called beliefs, thoughts, or memories. This idea runs counter to the teaching we have received in countries where our ancient Judeo-Christian traditions apply powerful pressure. In fact, we find it much easier to shove the responsibility for whatever might be unpleasant onto others and assume the role of victim. It seems much more comfortable.

Yet it really is not! Whatever happens, you are not a victim nor have you ever been one. You are the creator of 100 percent of what befalls you.

This is something that can really appear difficult to accept at first glance. Yet it is the key to the entire Ho'oponopono process. It is absolutely necessary to incorporate this idea entirely before beginning practice of Ho'oponopono in an effective manner.

An erroneous thought will create an erroneous reality, whereas if I have an accurate thought, I am creating a reality of harmony and peace. Here we need to grasp that everything is inside of us; there is nothing on the outside that we have not caused to be there.

 Physical reality is a creation of our thoughts; in other words, we participate in the creation of everything that happens to us.

This is a notion that is often quite difficult to accept and maintain. Up to this point we have been living with the idea that the responsible party is the other party, and the events we experience come to us, quite obviously, from the outside. With

Ho'oponopono the perspective is reversed. In reality, nothing has changed. Simply speaking, we were unaware that we had always unconsciously created our reality.

"Once something appears before you," said Dr. Len, "ask yourself what is happening inside you and around you—what you are in the midst of experiencing." It is then a matter of taking 100 percent responsibility for what you are feeling and in the process of creating. Next, once you have accepted this situation—which you have totally created—then you can launch the process of cleansing all the memories and beliefs that are causing your annoyance. Your memories cause irritation because they give you no respite. They rule your life at the unconscious level and prevent you from expressing your free will.

However, "We are not the sum of our memories; we are not our memories," as Morrnah Simeona said, "because we are more than that."

All that takes place in your life—events, meetings, where you live, journeys—is created by your memories. They are guiding your life by remote control. They cause you to believe that you are different from others, but in reality, they are the sole cause of the illusion of separation. This is why it is helpful to remind yourself that you are not your memories. This will lead you to ask that fundamental question that Morrnah raised, that Dr. Len raised, and which every human being has the right to raise: "Who am I really?"

Quite simply, your memories prevent you from being yourself, and by freeing yourself of that burdensome "heritage," by patiently stripping away the memories one after another as you would the skin of an onion, you will be guided into the discovery of who you truly are. In other words, everything that appears on the outside that disturbs you, sets you off balance, and causes you pain is a memory. The suffering you witness in another person is a memory that is being reactivated inside your own being.

Ho'oponopono permits you to clear away your memories. Memories are not intrinsically bad or good; we make that judgment about them. It may be that the memory of an event seemed good for years (for example, a marriage) but we now remember it as bad (it ended in divorce). Some memories appear to be false, and others seem accurate. However they are all only memories that need to be cleansed so you can be free of them. Ho'oponopono makes this possible.

The Different Parts of Your Identity

Memories are stored in the subconscious mind, which the Hawaiians call *unihpili,* or "inner child."* It is the headquarters of emotions and memories. In this part of the self where memories are stored, the inner child has great need of reassurance and love. It is for this reason that Ho'oponopono invites you to ask your inner child to release all fears and be freed of the memories that are the root cause of any troublesome problem or situation. It is this love you show your inner child that allows you to release old memories and lighten the load of this burden.

Furthermore, the conscious mind, or *uhane,* which means "mother"† for Hawaiians, is the part that represents the mind or intellect—that part of us that can choose either to cleanse the memories or to reject the process and thereby maintain

---

*The Hawaiian language is fluid, and one word can have several meanings. In this case, unihpili can also be translated as "unconscious mind" or "deity," both of which seem relevant.

†Also variously translated as "the soul," "dream," and "strong spirit."

the illusion of control. Its role is important. It requires much humility because in making the choice to cleanse the memories, the mind must let go of the reins. It must display trust by effacing itself before the divinity within.

Finally, the superconscious or soul, or even the superego, is what Hawaiians call *aumakua,* which means "father."* This is the part of consciousness that is in direct contact with the inner divinity and will request that you clean away memories once the subconscious mind has released them. The request is addressed to the superego, or soul, which immediately relays the request to the inner divinity, whose role is to cleanse and purify the cause or causes of the problem. It is also possible to address your inner divinity directly.

How Is This Cleansing Performed?

You will be using the four key phrases of Ho'oponopono, which are: "I'm sorry, forgive me, I thank you, I love you."

Regular practice of Ho'oponopono can eventually lead to an abbreviation of these phrases into a simple, "Sorry, forgive me, thanks, I love you," or even, "Thanks, I love you." Let your intuition guide you to use the words in a way that is best suited to you.

You begin with "I'm sorry," because you were unaware that you carried that memory inside of yourself. Then you say "Forgive me" to the divinity you carry within yourself, and ask the divinity for assistance in self-forgiveness that you allowed these memories to lead you astray. Next you thank the memories

_____

*Also variously translated as a "family god," "deified ancestor," or "ancestor reincarnated in a different form."

for appearing to you, and thus giving you the opportunity to free yourself of them. You also thank your inner divinity for helping you in this liberation.

You conclude by saying "I love you," because only love can heal. When you say this you are speaking to both your memories and to yourself.

The Ho'oponopono process is to forgive yourself, thank yourself, and send yourself love. By doing this, you erase the memory. As this suffering vanishes from within you, it also disappears from the other person. When you speak these words, you are addressing yourself, specifically the young child within you who is in pain.

 You have nothing to do or understand other than just to say these words.

This is the simplicity of Ho'oponopono. It is no longer necessary to hunt for the source of a disruptive memory—the painful event surrounding its origin. The process seems difficult to the mind only because the mind wants to control and understand everything.

But your mind is useful in this process and plays an important role. The mind has its own free will. It can make the decision to let go of all control and power, and place its trust in the inner divinity by asking your superego to clean out and thus free you of your memories.

This is why, when you enter into this Ho'oponopono energy, it is necessary to have developed great trust in yourself and a total faith in your soul to allow the mind to finally relinquish all its power and control. The intellect gives way to the intuition of the heart.

We could say that the mind is similar to a supercomputer, a computer so perfect that it would be impossible for humans ever to manufacture another as efficient. But even the best computer would be useless without software and data. It would be an empty machine.

The mind functions in much the same way as a computer; it uses your past memories for data. The mind always refers back to them before making any decision, which ensures that you conduct your life according to patterns dictated by the past. If you stop judging—in other words, cease using the recipes of the past—you will be living in the present moment and be prepared to welcome a new reality. This new reality will no longer be under the control of your ego but under the guidance of your soul.

Let Go of Expectations

The objective and main purpose of Ho'oponopono is to connect you to your inner divinity through your soul.

To do this you'll need to drop all expectations, because once you have embraced Ho'oponopono energy, it is no longer necessary to seek understanding or have expectations for any result. Being in a state of expectation does nothing but bring the mind back onto the scene.

When you are expecting anything, it means your mind has gotten involved. And once the mind seizes control, the soul will withdraw and nothing will happen. From that moment on, the mind will be working to block the process. It is therefore essential that the mind completely lets go of everything.

Letting go of expectations is very difficult, because it means not wanting anything. We have been taught to pursue and achieve our goals and interests by first understanding them through the study of data, then moving into action. We are accustomed to working this way. This puts us in the domain of the "reasonable," which depends on the intellect, the mind, and the ego. Furthermore the very choice of an objective is the fruit of the mind's reflection. This is how, generally speaking, most people operate.

To make its choice of a desired objective, the mind will draw from its databank of memories and past experiences, just as a computer takes data from its hard drive. Accordingly, the choice of an objective—making a decision—is most definitely nothing more than the product of our memories. This is how the mind can deceive itself so often.

The Empty State and the Present Moment

The mind exists only in the past or future, and loses its power and all control in the present moment. In the present, the mind relinquishes the reins. This is why the Ho'oponopono process knows only the specific present moment. The precondition for its effectiveness is to practice it in the present moment by disconnecting from the mind.

When you practice Ho'oponopono—I would even say when you "live" Ho'oponopono, for it is a state of mind—the letting go and detachment must be total in order to attain this state of emptiness, the "zero state" that Dr. Len mentions. The state of emptiness can only be reached in the here and now.

 It is in this state of emptiness and detachment that inspiration appears.

Inspiration comes from the soul of the indwelling divinity. The inner divinity knows exactly what is good for us. Inspiration is always on target.

Love of Self

It is important to always maintain this love energy at a higher level. To do this, meditate on these phrases daily. You can turn to the Ho'oponopono process for everything. Once you leave home to go to work or to a meeting, immediately ask your higher self or the divinity within to cleanse you of anything that could cause a problem or obstacle with the people you are going to meet.

 Repeat the phrases "Sorry, forgive me, thanks, I love you," and you will gradually see the magic work.

Leave it to your intuition to find the words and phrases that are most appropriate for you. Ask your inner child to release the memories, then thank your inner child with a reminder of your love. Offer reassurance.

Address your higher self by asking it to purify, with the help of the inner divinity, the causes of the problem; then thank it.

You can address your memories specifically by reminding them that you love them because they are giving you the opportunity of freeing them, thereby freeing yourself.

By practicing Ho'oponopono several times every day in this way, you will develop ever-increasing reserves of such magnificent values (that are like bits of love) as gratitude, forgiveness, the ability to let go, joy, humility, nonjudgment, faith in yourself, and self-esteem.

This is how you will gradually discover who you truly are.

The purpose of Ho'oponopono is to free yourself of your memories so that you can attain the light and illumination you need to know freedom and peace.

How to Practice Hoʻoponopono

Behind every event, situation, and encounter you experience in your life hides a memory. The goal of Hoʻoponopono is to free you of everything that can pose an obstacle in your life or be a source of pain, torment, and suffering.

The practice should carry you into a zero state of emptiness in which the mind has entirely surrendered control to your divine aspect. This makes it possible for you to be receptive to your inner divinity's message through what is commonly known as inspiration. The purpose is to remain in this state for as often as possible so that you can become permanently receptive and available.

The practice of Hoʻoponopono should become like a reflex action in your life. It is important to welcome everything, insignificant as it may seem, with feelings of gratitude, forgiveness, humility, and love.

There is no constraint involved with this, nor is there any effort to be made. This is because once you have made this practice a reflex, the words "I'm sorry, please forgive me, thank you, I love you" will automatically come into your mind or off your lips.

Speaking these words aloud is not an absolute obligation or a sine qua non condition. I regularly simply say, "Thank you, I love you," often repeating it several times. You can use the words that seem most suitable to you. Some people say "light," or "I accept," or even just "thank you."

Therefore, once anything unpleasant occurs, you can enunciate the full process in your mind or aloud: "I am entirely the creator of what happens and I accept this situation. I know that it is produced by a memory, and I have decided to free myself from it. So I am asking my inner child or my subconscious mind to let go of this memory and drop it. I am asking my soul, which is in contact with my inner divinity, to cleanse this memory so that it may be purified and transmuted into light." Throughout this whole process, it is important to always remain without any expectations concerning the final result.

In the practice, it is enough to simply say, "I'm sorry, forgive me, thank you, I love you," or "Thank you, I love you," knowing that these words embody the entire process.

Ho'oponopono is applicable to everything. You can begin cleaning your memories when you get up in the morning, thinking, for example, of your meetings over the course of the day, even if you don't know which ones might present an obstacle for you or be annoying. For each of these meetings say, "I'm sorry, forgive me, thank you, I love you," so that they transpire in the best possible way for you.

But you can also perform Ho'oponopono in the car, in the subway, at work, or when you are with your family or friends. Whenever a disturbing event occurs or a disagreement breaks out, this becomes a motive for cleansing, because they are all based on memories.

Practicing Ho'oponopono this way will illuminate your path. It is a permanent state of letting go. But in order to drop something, it is first necessary to take on the responsibility. Next comes acceptance, which is achieved by rising to a higher level where you can remember who you are. This is how you can decide to liberate this memory that is generally behaving in an unconscious manner. You then give the divine part of your being permission to exist, which will transmute the memory through love.

The Creative Power

Mahatma Gandhi, leader of India's nonviolent independence movement, wisely noted, "If we could change ourselves, the tendencies in the world would also change. As a man changes his own nature, so does the attitude of the world change toward him." Because the world is only the reflection of what we are, once we change, the world changes. We are the world; the world is us.

When something unpleasant occurs in your life, what is your instinctive reaction? You look outward to find the person at fault—the guilty party. This is something that seems so obvious you do not even question it. If the unpleasantness came from outside, responsibility for it must also be outside.

Furthermore, those who direct and influence our lives encourage us to keep our gaze continuously trained on the outside world. This leads us to see ourselves as victims and to believe that danger always comes from outside. Consequently we shed our responsibility for everything, and this is why doctors, teachers, employers, and neighbors are constantly being dragged into court for trivial matters. In health matters we have extremely practical scapegoats, such as viruses, tobacco, pollution, and many other things. Christian religions laid the groundwork long ago by inculcating in the faithful the idea that we are sinners at birth and live under the probing eye of a merciless God ever ready to punish us. The archetype of the victim has been deeply rooted in us, and this is convenient for such external powers as politicians and religious leaders, not to mention politicians with a religious agenda.

But what happens when you keep looking outside of yourself for the one responsible for your discomfort? You give away your power! Because the guilty party is somewhere else, you are giving that party your power and no longer have control over your life.

Conclusion: If an outside agent is responsible for your misfortune, that party has all power over you. Yet throughout our lives we continually place our power in the hands of others.

At this point you are almost certainly asking yourself, "If I am responsible for the situation that has so disturbed me, how can I resolve it?"

This is the moment when you recuperate your power because you now believe that nobody else is responsible for what happens to you. If you think you are the creator of everything that happens to you, then you have the power to change it. It is no longer somebody's fault; the person or situation has entered your life to show you what needs to be transformed for the better within you.

 In no case are others responsible; you are the sole person responsible for the things that happen in your life—all of them!

Once you have realized this, you can say: "You have no power over me or over my life. I am the craftsman of my own life. I am going to change whatever it is that caused something disruptive in my life or caused me to suffer. I am in control of my life."

When a problem crops up in your life, is its solution outside of you? If you want this problem to go away, must you try to change those who, according to you, are the causes of the problem that upset you? Let's look at the answer with the "overhead projector."

The Overhead Projector

Using the metaphor of an overhead projector—a device that projects images on a screen, one after the other—I am going to show you what it means to say that you "create your own reality every moment of your life," and also how a problem is often not located where we have become accustomed to believe it is.

Imagine that you are comfortably relaxing at a friend's house, watching a slide show. All at once something about a particular slide upsets you terribly. It might be a written phrase, or the depiction of a scene, a person, colors, or shapes, but it is not important to know. What is notable is that something in what you saw disturbed you so much that it triggered intense emotion. This emotion appears to be affecting you deeply because, all at once, in the grip of anger, you stand up and start toward the image. Then, picking up a sharp object, you slice apart the screen in a rage. But you see the image continues to be projected on the wall behind the screen. You then hurl yourself upon it, with the idea of destroying this image that has upset you so terribly.

If someone gave you a pickaxe to break apart the wall at the place on which the image was projected, would this be a good method for making the image disappear? Obviously not! Everyone knows that to change the image projected by an overhead projector, you need to simply change the slide inside it. Consequently, if an image projected by an overhead projector is upsetting you, the solution to the problem does not lie in the screen or the wall behind it but in the overhead projector itself.

It is enough to simply change the slide to obtain another image, only this time, one that does not upset you.

Do you think things work differently for you? Of course not, for every human being functions in some way just like this overhead projector. When a problem appears, you immediately start to look for the solution to this problem outside yourself, as if the causes of the problem were separate from you and had absolutely no connection with you. If you do this, you are definitely barking up the wrong tree, as the solution to every problem you encounter is not outside of you. In fact, any event that befalls you has no specific existence outside of yourself. The perception you have of it is only the reflection of your thoughts, beliefs, and memories.

 Like the overhead projector, you will find the solution to your problem not outside yourself but inside, and the cause of the problem has nothing to do with it.

You are, to some extent, an overhead projector, albeit one that is probably a thousand times more effective, for in the same way, you project images, scenes, and people who are only reflections of what you are inside, only reflections of your thoughts. You will recall how the more intense the emotions that accompany these thoughts were, the more creative were your thoughts. But where do your thoughts come from if not your memories? These are the thought-generating memories that Ho'oponopono, through a very simple procedure, offers you the opportunity to clean out so you can get free of the grip they have on your life and find peace.

Forgiveness Opens the Door to Love

The phrases "I'm sorry" and "please forgive me" form part of the Ho'oponopono process. A person could also say, "I am sorry because I did not know I had these memories inside me. Please forgive me, my inner child who has suffered so much and whom I abandoned; forgive me, my soul, for having withdrawn my trust in you; forgive me, my memories, for having ignored you. I ask forgiveness from myself for the suffering I have inflicted upon myself for lack of self-love, and forgiveness from others for judgments I made about them."

Customarily we believe we must forgive others for what they have done to us. The others are considered guilty and we are then judging them. But how can we judge others if they are only a reflection of ourselves? Judging others is judging ourselves.

Once you have become mired in judgment or criticism, you seal your heart to the omnipresent love that is the source of life, and you stop loving. Judgment brings about the duality and sense of separation that cuts you off from the energy of love. Once you cease to give love, you immediately penalize yourself, for you have severed your connection to love and can no longer receive it.

This is the time to ask, with feelings of great sincerity, forgiveness from those who "apparently" are the causes of all your inconveniences, because by judging them you have used them in a way that has severed you from love.

 Forgiveness is essential in the Ho'oponopono process because it frees you from your shadow zones and fears, and opens you to love.

The Light and the Shadow

Imagine for a moment that you are in a windowless room. There is a door but all the cracks have been perfectly caulked. The light is off and the room is completely dark. You are standing in this totally dark room with your hand resting on the doorknob. You know that on the other side of the door is another room that is perfectly lit and luminous.

All at once you pull open the door. What happens? You are probably dazzled but also observe that light has entered the room in which you have been standing. This is hardly a surprise and you regard it as completely normal. On the other hand, do you see any change in the extremely well-lit room? Has it become darker as it shared its light? Obviously not. This room that was so luminous remains so, and the luminosity remains unchanged. It is just as bright as it was the moment you opened the door.

These are questions that may seem absurd to you. It's completely obvious, you will tell yourself. And yet the darkness of the windowless room exists only because of the absence of light. Once light has been allowed to enter, the darkness is reduced, becoming less dark.

What does this mean? Can we say the dark does not exist? Science knows much about the properties of light, its composition, speed, and so on. We have far less information about the dark.

Darkness appears to be the reverse of light—its opposite. In the same way that darkness can exist only because of the absence of light, we can also say that our fears exist only because of the absence of love.

Light is everywhere and always; in the same manner, love, too, is everywhere. It is within everything and forms an integral part of everything that exists. Your fears are shadow zones—your dark regions.

Let's go back to our metaphor and imagine that you are still in the dark room with your hand on the doorknob. The door is slightly ajar for many people, and a little more open for others. But why don't you open that door wide so you can bathe in the light? Why are you so tightly gripping the doorknob, preventing it from opening wider to love? Why do you cling to your fears and continue to shut yourself away from love? It is difficult to break away from your habits, memories, and recollections. You are accustomed to them and know them well, even if they are synonymous with various episodes of pain and suffering. You hold on to them out of laziness, fear of change, or fear of the unknown.

Actually, if the path of love has not been revealed to you, if someone has not taught you how to love yourself or just simply to love, then true love can be a source of fear. It may seem paradoxical to say this. However, it is easy to understand that everything you do not hold within is an unknown, and the unknown inspires fear. If love were not a natural part of you, you could never attract love.

Yet it seems so easy to just twist that doorknob and thus allow yourself to be permeated by love. To do this you will need to develop within yourself the ability to let go and trust in your soul. It is not a question of opening the door too violently, because being dazzled can be painful. You will do it in accordance with your own rhythm, your own particular pace of development.

 Absolute forgiveness can lead us to this state of letting go that will free us. As Colin Tipping remarks in *Radical Forgiveness*, "True forgiveness must include letting go completely of victim consciousness."[1]

Total Forgiveness

For minds that have been deeply conditioned by Judeo-Christian principles, forgiveness is a delicate concept because it confines us in the notion of guilt. We think, "If I ask forgiveness, it is because I am guilty of some transgression." The ego is reluctant to acknowledge its mistake and even more reluctant to ask forgiveness.

This is why getting out of the grip of heavy memories that have been inculcated over centuries is no easy matter. Furthermore, there is something humiliating about acknowledging guilt and transgressions. But once humiliation has been transformed into humility, then forgiveness can liberate you entirely from the role of victim by inviting you to radically alter your vision of the world, as well as your interpretation of everything that happens to you.

In the practice of Ho'oponopono, at the moment you are saying, "Forgive me," or "Please forgive me," address this forgiveness to yourself. At this moment you will attain the ultimate power that forgiveness can give you. It will lead you into a feeling of indescribable happiness, a liberating sense of relief, and a complete state of release. The door of your heart will finally open without effort, and you will be suffused and transported by light. It is like being reborn.

We can look at forgiveness as the central axis of the Ho'oponopono process. If the request for forgiveness is made with great sincerity and in a state of profound humility, then fears and resistance can start to dissolve and make way for total love. Forgiveness is truly a door that allows you to get beyond the grip of the ego and closer to that infinite space of freedom and peace, which is that of the heart.

It is through this gift that you make yourself "one" with

the Divine Source. In the words of Olivier Clerc, in *The Gift of Forgiveness,* "In choosing to ask for forgiveness, we move from a place of self-importance and pride to a place of humility. We drop our pretense, climb down from our ivory tower, and something opens up inside us. By shedding our armor and our grievances, we are free again."[2]

The Golden Buddha

Love is everywhere. It assures the cohesion and unity of all things, of the universe, of all living organisms, and of ourselves, whether or not we are aware of it.

 All is love; you are love.

So what then is preventing you from gaining access to this wonderful treasure you hold within your being? It is your fears. Fears are a construction of the ego that acts like a protective shell or disguise you use to display your face to the world.

Let's illustrate this with a story that took place in Thailand. In 1957 a group of monks was entrusted with the task of moving a giant clay Buddha statue from one temple to another. Their monastery in Bangkok was scheduled to be moved to permit construction of a highway. They needed a crane to lift this enormous Buddha, and as it was hoisted, cracks began appearing in the clay. Then it began to rain. Mindful of keeping the statue safe, the monks stood it back down on the ground and covered it with a large tarp to protect it.

During the night, the abbot went to check on the condition of the Buddha. When he turned on a flashlight to see if the statue had remained dry, he saw a brilliant reflection coming from the cracks in the clay. This intrigued him, and taking a closer look, he saw that the clay appeared to be hiding something. He immediately went to find a hammer and chisel and when he returned, he began removing pieces of clay from the cracked areas. As the abbot's work progressed and pieces of clay continued to fall from the statue, the Buddha became more and more lustrous.

The abbot worked the entire night, and when he'd removed every single layer of clay that covered the statue, a magnificent, massive gold Buddha was revealed.

Historians believe that several centuries earlier, at the time the Burmese Army was preparing to invade what was then Siam (which later became Thailand and neighboring countries), the monks were warned of the imminent attack and, anxious to protect their valuable Buddha from pillage, had covered it with a thick layer of clay. Because all the monks were slain during the attack, the Buddha was left abandoned and its well-guarded secret was not discovered until 1957.

 For centuries this Buddha had shown its coarse yet solid shell, hiding its treasure within.

This is a splendid and highly symbolic story for it shows that you, like this gold Buddha, are covered by a shell that has been entirely created by your ego and prompted by your fears.

The Cleansing of Memories

You generally detest the layer of clay that covers you, this carapace made from your fears, beliefs, and memories. However, you will undoubtedly acknowledge that the Buddha in this story owed love and infinite gratitude to his clay shell for protecting him from pillaging for so many years.

Similarly, you should tame, then love, your fears, for their hidden faces reveal a treasure. Wouldn't your individual mission be to remove your protective shell, to take off this veil that hides your true nature and prevents you from discovering your true self?

When seen this way, your shell appears like the keeper of a divine message that will help guide you through your own development. It has fulfilled its role to this point, the role of protecting you. It is by exploring every facet of all your fears that you can gradually unveil the pure love that forms your holy essence.

The abbot used a hammer and chisel, but you have wonderful tools at your disposal. With Hoʻoponopono you are going to clean away these "layers of clay" that are your memories.

 In the space of a night, the monk laid bare the vast gold interior of the Buddha. All of life is a gift to you.

Reinforce your patience and trust in yourself. Your gratitude and love toward others, and the daily practice of Hoʻoponopono, will gradually free you from the unhealthy grip of your memories and help you discover, as you evolve, your own inner treasure. This treasure is the light being you truly are.

Love Is in Unity

The universe can be imagined as a large puzzle. Every plant, every living being, you, me, each planet, everything that exists constitutes one of the pieces of this puzzle. Every component is thus only a morsel of this "all" that we call universal energy, universal love, Source, or God. The name you give it doesn't matter. Each of these pieces is essential to the composition of the whole. Just as each zone of shadow and light is indispensable to the construction of your individual integrity, every living being is essential for the composition of the universal energy.

If a beam of white light is projected on a glass prism, the light refracts and reemerges transformed into a rainbow. If the operation is reversed and a colored light is projected on the prism, all the colors will merge together to form a white light. In order to obtain this white light again, it is necessary for every light that forms the spectrum to be present. If we imagine that a single vibration is removed from all of these colors, even the tiniest fragment, the same process will not provide a completely white light.

Imagine that every human being is one of these colors. We can then see that if a single person is rejected or set aside because he is unloved, humanity will not completely attain perfect, unconditional love, because we are all connected, united as one in a single energy that is love.

 Accept others as being part of yourself.

Each human being must also recognize and accept all the facets that make up his or her totality, including hatred, anger, greed, joy, peace, and so forth.

White is not the absence of color; to the contrary, it is the blend of all the colors. In the same way, love is the whole of all your values and all your shadow zones; it encompasses everything.

There is no good or evil, no more than there are defects or virtues. There are simply your memories that conceal the sparkling light being you truly are.

2

From the Psychological World to Quantum Reality

Luc Bodin, M.D.

Understanding your emotional and psychological blocks is the first step in getting rid of them. Until you know something is an obstacle to your growth, you have no incentive for removing it. In fact, you may have no idea it even exists.

False Memories Explained by Neuro-Linguistic Programming (NLP)

Do not be scared of moving forward too slowly; fear only stopping.

CHINESE PROVERB

Ho'oponopono is often explained in lectures as a technique for eliminating "false memories" that are responsible for the unpleasant situations that arise in daily life. In this way Ho'oponopono frees you of the ball and chains you are lugging around, often without even being aware you are doing so, which cloud your judgment and often stop you dead in your tracks.

Just what these false memories are never gets truly explained in these lectures. However, it seems important to get acquainted with their origins, not only to understand their active mechanisms, but also to fully comprehend why it is important to erase them.

Neuro-Linguistic Programming,* a set of personal development and communication techniques more commonly known as NLP, makes it possible to grasp the origins of these

---

*Neuro-Linguistic Programming, formulated by John Grinder and Richard Bandler in the 1970s, offers tools designed to remove blockages and surmount personal difficulties.

disruptive memories. NLP explains that all your positions in life, all your decisions and choices, are directly connected to your values—what you consider important enough that it governs your life; and beliefs—what you accept as fact, even in the absence of proof. If, for example, business success is important to you, the decisions you make will not be the same as those of a person who mostly desires to please others and be liked.

 Like everyone, you hold beliefs and values that you regard as essential rules for living. Most of these come from your parents and your earliest childhood, but they can be altered, transformed, or erased over the course of your life, depending on your experiences and the people you meet.

To you these values and beliefs are as self-evident as "the sky is blue" or "grass is green." However, they are entirely subjective and differ wildly from one individual to the next. They are so deeply rooted in you that you are no longer even aware of their subjective nature. Initially they were only postulates, but little by little they transformed into what you perceive as fundamental elements, and they run your life. These may be, for example, respect for one's word, belief in God, the importance of honesty or good manners, the necessity of power, family, work, money, fame, or recognition, and so forth. All these postulates gradually turned into fundamental mechanisms that work automatically and often unconsciously, and they constitute a large part of your memories.

A large number of them could be wrong or limiting, if not outright delusional. These are the false memories that lead to unreliable decisions and aberrational behavior. This all happens because your vision of the world has been distorted by a filter constructed from irrational values or beliefs. For example, if you think the world is conspiring against you and is seeking your destruction, you will have great difficulty leaving your house to go to the movies, travel, or simply meet other people, which will obstruct you greatly in your daily life, as well as in your personal development.

Added to these deceptive beliefs and values are the fears that will also greatly restrict your activities and decisions. These elements are the source of the majority of your erroneous memories.

Let's now take a much closer look at what this involves.

Fears

Your fears* derive primarily from the fears of your parents and those close to you (other family members, teachers, friends) who pass them down, often unknowingly, in the erroneous belief that they are protecting you. This is how they transmit their vision of the world and what happens in it to the next generation. All parents, even the most attentive, fall prey to this tendency.

For example, telling a child not to be scared of a storm in order to give reassurance actually programs the child to be frightened. No one ever says, "Don't be scared of that apple," or, "Don't be scared of that cloud in the sky." The simple phrase "Don't be scared" immediately sends the child a message that there is some reason to be frightened in this situation, whereas the parent thinks that saying this will reassure the child and divert the threatening thought from the child's mind.

But this can take place in a much more subtle fashion

---

*Fear: an unpleasant, often strong emotion caused by anticipation or awareness of danger (Merriam-Webster). This danger can be either real or imaginary.

without using spoken language. Children are also very quick to perceive nonverbal cues. They pick up their parents' fears just by being aware of their attitudes. For example, a parent might have fear of being in a large crowd in a department store, or driving on a bridge. Without even a word being said, the child records it and incorporates it into future behavior patterns.

Fears can also be formed over the course of a lifetime, depending on the individual's personal experiences. Accidents, grief, losing a job, separations, and assaults are all situations that can weaken or destabilize an individual and be a source of later fears of car accidents, losing a child, being fired, being abandoned by a spouse or lover, and so on.

Fears can get in the way of living a satisfying life and achieving fulfillment.

Values

Values also play a direct role in the direction and organization of your endeavors. Everyone has at least five or six that provide the foundations on which you manage your life. The drawback is that some of these values can be limiting or inadaptable, thus blocking your development (such as an overly rigid doctrine) or distorting your reality (for example, "Always be nice").

This was the case with a young woman who had been programmed in childhood with the "be nice" value. Her mother constantly cajoled her with statements such as, "Oh Sylvia, if you were nice, you would go buy me bread at the bakery," or, "Sylvia, be a nice girl and fetch my glasses that I left in the dining room." Repeated daily, these short phrases created a golden rule for this woman: "Always be nice" to everyone! This created many problems in her life as an adult woman, for she did not know how to say no. Her excessive niceness led her to marry three men for whom she had no particular feeling of love (she never dared tell them no), which led to three successive divorces, followed by a life in painful solitude. At least this was the case until the day she realized that all these situations were the fruit of an erroneous memory she carried inside—that of always needing to be nice. Ho'oponopono helped her get rid of this limiting value so that she could begin being herself. She began to feel really alive and her relationship problems were resolved.

Most of our values come from our parents. They are most often a blend of both parents' values, because of course we always try to please them to get their approval, even if we are completely unaware that we are doing so. But some values we develop all on our own based on life experiences.

Beliefs

Beliefs are unverified and often unverifiable pieces of information that we nonetheless believe to be true. We mostly learn them from parents, family, close friends, or teachers. But as with our values, other beliefs are constructed over the course of our lives in accordance with the successes and failures we experience and the kinds of situations we encounter.

Beliefs are elements we use to grasp and shape our lives. There is, for example, the belief that the world is a dangerous place, or that you should never show your emotions, or are worthless. Or perhaps you believe in divine justice or reincarnation. A belief changes the way you see and understand life. For example, a number of years ago French singer Johnny Hallyday had a popular song with these lyrics: "I have a problem, I really feel I love you." This message was imprinted in the minds of many young people as "I love you = a problem," which does not encourage a healthy love life.

However, beliefs can take on many different guises. One of the most familiar is that of religious belief; the individual has no proof whatsoever that God exists or does not exist, but he has faith and this faith is indestructible. You need only consider the number of people killed throughout the ages in the name of religion. This shows just how powerful beliefs can be.

Fears, values, and beliefs are therefore subjective elements, present in you, that direct your life and destiny. They also condition your thoughts and thus, through the law of attraction, attract situations that correspond to them, which is to say, situations that are of the same nature.

Harmonious beliefs and values will attract situations that are beneficial for you and for your development. On the other hand, fears, or distorted values or beliefs, will attract into your life precisely the situations you were hoping to avoid, and thus create extremely unpleasant events.

Fears, values, and beliefs are what Ho'oponopono calls "erroneous memories."

Looking at the problem from the opposite angle, if you are going through an unpleasant situation it generally means there is an inappropriate fear, value, or belief (erroneous memory) behind it. By becoming aware of this, you have the choice of keeping it or getting rid of it. You might believe your value of "honesty" is good, and one you'd like to keep. You may find yourself believing that the fear you have of the world around you is appropriate, and that it's a good idea to keep it. You may think that your belief that you are worthless is normal and is a good thing to remember.

This is where your free will comes into play.

But you may also consider that these are all filters that distort your vision of life and your judgment, and thus they act as brakes, if not obstacles, to your personal development and self-fulfillment. You may also wish to eliminate the unpleasant situation. If this is the case, you can decide to erase any memories you deem erroneous or disruptive by doing Ho'oponopono and using the energy of love.

Contentious Situations

When an inner situation is not made conscious, it happens outside, as fate.

PSYCHIATRIST CARL G. JUNG

Conflicts,* meaning worries, irritations, problems, inconveniences, or anxieties for self or others, are frequent occurrences over a lifetime. They always unfold in two stages.

The Phase of Active Conflict
This is the period of time when a solution has not yet been found for the problem. It is constantly present and being turned over and over in your mind. All your attention is concentrated on it, which tends to make it grow larger—so much so that you ignore everything else going on around you. This obsession provides absolutely no help in putting your problem into perspective, and

---

*We should not take the word *conflict* to mean *combat*. We are using it here in the sense of "a situation that poses a problem." For example, a conflict with your spouse does not necessarily mean having an argument. It can also arise out of a concern you have regarding your partner's health, problems at work, or something else.

it is of no assistance whatsoever in devising a solution. This is how a conflict can last for months, years, or even an entire lifetime.

In this situation it is best to first put some distance between yourself and your problem, for example, by thinking about something pleasant (vacations, outings, leisure activities, hobbies), and also by becoming aware that you and you alone have created this situation. It is the fruit of your erroneous memories, and Ho'oponopono can effectively help you get rid of it if you so desire. All it needs is for *you* to change and then the *situation* will change. You no longer have to wait for others to change. You are the true master of your own life.

The Phase of Conflict Resolution
This is the second stage. The individual has found within, possibly thanks to Ho'oponopono, the necessary resources to surmount a problem or find a solution to it. This is a phase of convalescence and recuperation, which is often accompanied by fatigue and temporary ailments.

However, some resolved conflicts can leave behind psychological aftereffects, just as is the case for certain illnesses of a physical nature. These aftereffects can even program new beliefs, new fears, or new values, of which a certain number can again be disruptive and the source of erroneous memories. For example, being laid-off from a job in a bad economy can eventually be accepted but is still destabilizing, and it may lead to self-depreciation and a constant fear of being laid off again by a subsequent employer. Here, too, Ho'oponopono can help overcome these disruptive feelings.

Ho'oponopono can step in as a liberating influence during a conflict by both erasing the erroneous memory that caused this problem and erasing new erroneous memories that otherwise will be created as a consequence of the event. We can describe them as erroneous memories created by erroneous memories. This shows how easy it is for these kinds of situations to grow more convoluted and intricate over time.

For example, a person has been laid off several times because of a belief (erroneous memory) that she or he is worthless. These repeated layoffs can generate within this individual new erroneous memories, such as fear of being laid off again, fear of not having enough money, and even the fear that the world is a wicked place, and so forth. This is how new erroneous memories are formed following the occurrence of events prompted by an old erroneous memory. This can be the origin of an endless series of chain reactions.

This is why when an unpleasant event occurs, Ho'oponopono must be performed several times in order to erase *all* the memories connected to it. Dr. Len performed Ho'oponopono in his office every day over his patients' case files, but it took several months before the improvement of his patients could be observed.

 Numerous erroneous memories can lie concealed behind a difficult situation. It is only when all these memories have been erased that the situation will start to improve.

The Cycle of Conflicts

Seek not to change the world, but choose to change your mind about the world.

JESHUA, *A COURSE IN MIRACLES*

You may have noticed that the unpleasant situations you experience in your life—a series of layoffs, repeated breakups, money problems, or setbacks in your studies—have a vexing tendency to repeat themselves. This can give you the impression that life has it in for you and is actively working against you. In fact, it is nothing of the kind. The cause is not that the universe has evil intentions toward you, but certain fears, beliefs, or values that you carry disrupt your thoughts and thereby summon—through resonance—unpleasant situations that mirror them. Because you remain stuck within the same negative thought patterns, you continue to attract the same contentious situations. It is simply logical.

This is why, instead of being a bolt of lighting from a clear blue sky, a conflict generally has precedents—past conflicts of the same kind that you ignored and therefore failed to resolve. Because the erroneous memory has not been erased, it continues to be active and to summon new but identical situations, which sets up a "cycle of conflicts."

The Personal Cycle of Conflicts

This mechanism explains why you ceaselessly re-create the same kind of contentious situation. Your erroneous memory generally began by causing a series of minor unpleasant incidents in your life, such as annoyances, vexations, or small setbacks. These incidents were quickly forgotten and, quite often, you did not trouble yourself about identifying their cause. The erroneous memory was therefore able to remain very much alive in your mind. Some time later, it again produced a situation of the same type, probably more unpleasant than its predecessor—and if it was ignored again . . . It may have grown hazy over time as the problem again vanished. But the memory is still there. It will subsequently generate new conflicts that are always a bit stronger than the preceding ones. Over the years, if left ignored, they will become increasingly violent and powerful, until they trigger such dramatic events as divorce, an accident, or serious illness.

> The solution obviously consists, then, in becoming aware of the fact that these repeated conflicts are the work of an erroneous memory within, and that it will be necessary to erase it in order to put an end to these repeated conflicts.

For example, a young woman has been married and divorced twice for the same reason: her husband beat her. After her second divorce she began spending time with a young man who also started beating her after they had been together for a while. Disgusted by men, she began a life of celibacy, living alone with her son—who eventually started beating her. All these situations were generated by an erroneous memory this woman was holding within, and this memory had to be erased if she wanted to see no further repetition of this situation in her life ever again. (Her erroneous memory is, of course, not an excuse for the attitude or actions of these men!)

If, instead of waiting for tragedy, the memory had been eliminated at the time of the first annoying incidents, it would have avoided a lot of setbacks and disappointment. This is why it is important to do Ho'oponopono for all unpleasant and disagreeable incidents that arise in your life, whether a simple heartache, an annoyance, the reawakening of a bad memory, a sorrow, an unpleasant thought, some bad news, or anything that causes distress. The effacement of the memory will prevent its return later in a more unpleasant and more violent form.

These conflicts often return in a cyclical fashion, with a regularity that will be different depending on the situations and the individuals. Every time, although the situation is different, the conflicts are always of the same nature, although as noted above, they are always more violent than before. It is as if the increasingly extreme nature of the repeated situation is intended to force awareness of an erroneous memory that needs to be resolved.

The Origin of the First Conflict

The first conflict of one of these cycles can occur at any moment in an individual's lifetime. In the majority of cases it starts in childhood, even in infancy. This is why we often find children who are beaten by their schoolmates or suffer failure at school; or the opposite—they are bullies and troublemakers who generate the violence.

But the origin of the first conflict can go far back in time, back to the day of birth or even before that to something suffered during life in the womb. This kind of conflict is much more frequent that one might think.

During pregnancy (*in utero*), the child feels everything its mother experiences: couple problems, physical or mental acts of violence, fears, grievances—the fetus records everything. Furthermore, once the pregnancy has been discovered, some couples will question whether or not they want to keep the child. This causes a terrible trauma for the child and will in turn generate fears. If one parent did not want the child, this is also a source of disruptive fears, values, and beliefs.

The birth, in addition to its physically traumatic aspect for both mother and child, constitutes the first separation conflict for the newborn as it represents separation from the mother who was the infant's entire world during pregnancy. During this period she assured the child love, food, warmth, and protection. Subsequently, over the course of the new being's life, separation conflict will be frequently renewed—to go to daycare or school, to go to work, to marry or divorce, and to survive the death of the parents.

 In this way the first conflicts, and thus the first erroneous memories, can arise from intrauterine life or the event of birth. These situations can even arise with great frequency.

But the origin of the cycle of conflicts can go back to an even earlier period of time. Let's take a look at how this can happen in the next section.

The Familial Cycle of Conflicts

A number of authors, for example, Anne Ancelin Schützenberger and Paola Del Castillo, have discovered a familial origin to numerous conflicts.[1] Their research has given birth to what is now called psychogenealogy.* It is true that situations often repeat through the generations—breast cancer, divorce at the same age, bankruptcy, and so on, which gives the impression that erroneous memories have been passed down from father to son or from mother to daughter.

Several elements can support—or explain, to be more precise—this theory of the familial cycle of conflicts. First, we have our inherited DNA, which comes from our parents and, through them, our earlier ancestors. But this does not mean

---

*Professor Anne Ancelin Schützenberger of the University of Nice developed a theory that events, traumas, and conflicts that were experienced by our ancestors, even those no longer living, shape the psychological disorders, illnesses, and behavior patterns we can't otherwise explain.

we should overlook the education given by the parents that transmits to the child, as we have seen, their fears, values, and beliefs, and therefore their erroneous memories. This is how the innate sense acquired through family heredity and the sense acquired through parental education can largely explain the occurrence of identical situations for children that previously occurred to their parents or grandparents.

We will look later at the field of epigenetics, a recent discovery in the field of genetics that shows how the expression of genes can be influenced by lifestyle choices and experiences. Epigenetics explains how our ancestors' experiences altered their genes, which were then passed down to succeeding generations. The phenomenon of epigenetics allows us to grasp the importance of genetics in familial cycles of conflict.

If we take the example of breast cancer that affected first a mother, then her daughter several decades later, there are several possible explanations for this phenomenon.

- The presence of cancerous genes that were passed on from the mother to her daughter, perhaps the hereditary genes BRCA1 and BRCA2.
- Identical living habits, taught by parents to children from infancy: diet, alcohol, tobacco, athletic activities, and so forth.
- An identical way of thinking, also inculcated since infancy: this is good, this is bad, you are nice, you are stupid, and so forth, which are the seeds for fears, values, and beliefs. What is involved here is a kind of "family filter" through which the child will perceive the world his entire life.

- Children's mimicry of their parents. This can be seen in adulthood by identical professions and attitudes, alcoholic parent and child, mother and daughter who divorce at the same age, and so on. The child grown into adulthood unconsciously re-creates the same situations experienced by the parents (often at the same ages), both desirable and not.

Although we cannot state the exact reason why this young woman was afflicted by the same kind of cancer as her mother, this problem has clearly been handed down from one generation to the next.

Another example is given us by Louise, who had not been able to find her life partner but decided to have a child. She chose a biological father and then raised the child by herself. Several years later, when drawing up her family tree, she was surprised to learn she had a great aunt, also named Louise, who had been a single mother. She then came across the same phenomenon again in an older generation, and another ancestor who also was a single mother. It turns out that three women in this family (two of whom share the same first name) raised a child on their own. It is difficult, in this case, to talk about coincidence.

According to psychogenealogy, it is primarily the last seven generations that influence the heredity of an individual and can thereby transmit their erroneous memories to their descendants. The memories of the older generations have arguably been erased, as if diluted by time. This seems logical, otherwise we would all have to go back to either Adam and Eve (whose transgressions many insist will always be a burden on us) or our earliest evolutionary ancestors, depending on what we believe about our origins.

Among the seven generations that influence us, the most predominant in this regard is that of the grandparents, perhaps even more so than the parents.

It also happens quite frequently that a kind of "family contract" exists in the familial unconscious, which would assign a particular position or mission to the just-born child, such as taking care of his brothers and sisters, or forming a bond among all the members of the family, or caretaking elderly parents or grandparents. Salomon Sellam gives us another example in his book *Le Syndrome du Gisant*.* He explains that numerous children find themselves burdened with a responsibility by the family contract of a recently deceased family member, such as an uncle killed in battle, or a sibling who died in an accident. The very choice of name predisposes the newborn to this assignment: Gisèle (*git-s-elle*, "here she lies"), Renè (*re-nait*, "reborn"). The newborn child is the unknowing receiver of a burden that is more or less unconsciously imposed by the family. This often translates into a task that the so-named child takes on reluctantly and with difficulty. But on the day such a person becomes aware of the weight imposed by the birth family, life becomes brighter and more colorful and the world suddenly seems full of possibility.

 Ho'oponopono will also be able to help in erasing this memory, for though it appears to have been engineered by the family of origin, it remains nonetheless true that the individual is still the architect of this situation.

**Le Syndrome du Gisant—un subtil enfant de remplacement* [The recumbent figure syndrome—a subtle replacement child]. The *gisant* typically refers to the prone effigy figure carved on a tomb.

It is, moreover, disconcerting to note that the simple fact of discovering a familial cause for a conflict—which is often a family secret, but also the familial erroneous memory—frequently is enough on its own to understand it and then resolve the conflict. This is because the discovery acts to some extent as a genuine revelation. It is as if the person always knew the answer to the problem but refused to see it. So when the familial cause is brought to the surface and put into words, the person immediately feels in a deep place that it is the truth and that now anything is possible. The person now wants just one single thing: to be freed of this contract and liberated from this familial erroneous memory. In some way the individual has done Ho'oponopono without even realizing it.

This is how conflicts, situations, and problems tend to repeat themselves from one generation into the next and so on. They will repeat again and again until one link of this family chain provides a solution to this conflict—the erroneous memory—thereby breaking the infernal cycle. This will simultaneously free the ancestors of the burden and spare the children from having to face the same kind of problem.

The Cycle of Previous Lives and Karma

Going back even further in time, for those who believe in reincarnation—and this includes a vast majority of those living on the planet—it is possible to discover the origin of the cycle of conflict in one's previous lives. For what it's worth, noted biologist and physicist Jacqueline Bousquet believes the reality of reincarnation can be proven mathematically.

Many researchers—notably the renowned Patrick Drouot and American psychiatrist Brian Weiss—have used techniques similar to hypnosis[2] to guide individuals back into their previous lives. The results can be quite disturbing, as was the case for the man who discovered that the origin of his asthma stemmed from his death in a gas chamber during a previous life. Someone else realized that her chronic chest pains came from the dagger that had stabbed and killed her in an earlier life.

In the same way, your problems in your current life could be the consequence of your conduct in another life. This is known as "karmic responsibility." In other words, if you behaved badly toward the poor and indigent in a previous life, you will be reborn as one of them in the next life. If you cheated on your spouse in one life, you will be the deceived husband or wife in the next.

This is, of course, a very simplified explanation. In reality, things are often much more subtle. But according to the law of "karma," the law of causes and consequences, every action you take in your life will have consequences on your karma, and therefore on the situations that befall you in later lives. When you grasp this karmic law, the saying "Do unto others as you would have done unto you" takes on its full meaning and is actually a fairly self-serving piece of advice. This counsel offers the best way of preserving your (good) karma and therefore your future in your next incarnation.

A karmic burden can be the source of an erroneous memory in your present life, which will be the cause of unpleasant situations. You will keep reliving it in life after life until you have finally found a solution for it, or erased it. Thank you, Ho'oponopono!

You Are the Only Creator

The origin of repetitive conflicts can be found in the past of your current life, in your previous lives, or even in the lives of your ancestors. But in truth, the origin of the problem is of scarce importance. It is not essential to know it with Ho'oponopono.

This is because, in all respects, it is you who are the creator of everything that happens in your life. It is you who chose the family into which you were born, the one that corresponds precisely to your karma, will allow you to answer the question you pose for yourself, and will generate the conflict you were not able to resolve in your past life. Let me repeat, it is you who are the creator of this situation. All you need to do is resolve it and thus eliminate this karmic burden and continue your evolution.

 You have personally chosen the ideal situation for creating the conflict.

What Purpose Do Conflicts Serve?

A situation is contentious because it touches one of your nerves, which is to say, one of your weak spots. For example, if you feel dislike for someone for no apparent reason, it is because that person represents for you, unconsciously, an aspect of yourself that you deny or do not like.

The conflict, the unpleasant situation, the problem arises in your life to reveal to you that aspect of your personality you have no desire to see. If you are unable to settle it, life will impose the same conflict upon you on a regular basis—cyclically—with increasing force until you are ready to accept the fact that you need to pay attention to it, in this life or the next.

The conflict exists to compel you to work on this part of yourself that you dislike, once and for all. Its solution or elimination will allow you to get rid of a block that is preventing your personal development. This is why, when you solve a problem or resolve a psychological conflict, you will come out of it changed, even transformed, and your personal evolution can then resume where it has been obstructed.

It is Ho'oponopono's admirable quality to offer very simple solutions for conflicts. By accepting that they are your creation—whatever their origin—and erasing them and transforming yourself, you will cause them to vanish permanently.

The Memory of Events

To know is not to demonstrate or explain. It is to gain access to vision.

ANTOINE DE SAINT-EXUPÉRY

Every day you live through multiple experiences. Millions of pieces of information enter your brain daily. You must select what you will keep in your memory and what you will erase. At least this is the belief of conventional medicine.

During sleep the brain memorizes those memories it will keep and eliminates the others. While you are in this period of rest your body does not need to expend energy on its activities of walking, digestion, concentration, movements, and so on, and can therefore concentrate all its energy on restoring the body and the management of memories.

Sleep allows the brain to consolidate what it has learned and integrate information into long-term memory. Only relevant, useful, or important bits of information are retained and the rest is jettisoned to make room for the information that will come in the following day. This is the conventional medical account of what transpires during sleep, but it may not be entirely accurate.

Sleep Cycles

A night of sleep consists of four to six cycles, each of which is comprised of four stages.

- Light sleep or wakeful relaxation consisting of alpha waves (8–13 Hz).
- Slow, light sleep characterized by theta waves (4–7 Hz), the phase during which the sleeper loses contact with his environment.
- Slow, deep sleep characterized by very slow delta waves (0.5–4 Hz). This is the deepest period of sleep. This stage contributes to the management of information that will be subsequently dealt with during paradoxical sleep.
- Paradoxical sleep, which is characterized by theta, then alpha waves. Dreams are intense during this time and consist of around 65–70 percent of fragments (memories, information, experiences) from the previous day and 30–35 percent from the two previous days. It is a very important stage for long-term memory, emotional management, and mental equilibrium.

During the 1980s I participated in experiments in sophrology* at the Center of Behavioral and Psychological Orientation in Paris, which showed that all the events of a life are retained in the human memory.

For example, a sixty-year-old man was able to recall, with

---

*Sophrology is a technique that acts on the levels of consciousness to induce physical or behavioral changes.

great precision, how he was dressed on the day he took his first steps, what he had for breakfast, what he had done that day, and so on. When the mind and consciousness are short-circuited during a sophrology session, it is easier to observe our phenomenal memory capacity. In such altered states of consciousness it is possible to see that the individual has preserved every bit of information gleaned during one or multiple lifetimes, from the most minor and insignificant to the most traumatizing.

This total memory is therefore present but not necessarily in the brain; you do not have direct access to it as you do to the habitual memory you use on a daily basis. Nor do you still have access, for example, to the history lessons you learned by heart when you were in high school. However, they are still there somewhere, inscribed in your memory.

Given this phenomenal memory capacity made available in sophronic states, it is logical to think that all these little annoyances, resentments, and minor frustrations you have experienced but no longer remember consciously are still present in the folds of your memory, where they can be the cause of erroneous memories that require elimination.

Psychology and Ho'oponopono

You must live as you think, otherwise you will end up thinking as you have lived.

PAUL BOURGET

Psychology takes an intense interest in the functioning of human psychic phenomena, which is to say, the mental life. Scientific research distinguishes between inside the human mind—a conscious mind that allows you to perceive your existence and the outside word—and an unconscious mind that represents the hidden side of the psyche, the submerged part of the iceberg. We all believe it is our conscious mind that makes choices and decisions, and organizes our lives. However, according to psychologists, the mind that customarily directs us is not the one we think.

 Realize that it is not your conscious mind that is sitting in the pilot's seat, but rather your unconscious mind, your hidden side.

Let's now take a look at how the mind manages a traumatic event in your life. The memory of the trauma will, during the early stages, continue to haunt your mind until you digest it, accept it, or find a solution to it. But if there is no solution to be found, or if the emotional shock is too painful and/or persists for too long, the mind will take action to relieve the mental tension by displacing the conflict toward the dungeons; in other words, the unconscious. The vexing thing about this automatic mechanism is that the conflict is never actually resolved. It remains active and continues generating anxiety. The problem then is that you feel anxious but no longer know why, which is the inevitable reaction since the conflict is now buried in your subconscious.

Caution!

It is obvious that in serious cases or in cases of extreme psychological disorders, Ho'oponopono will not replace the existing technologies of psychiatry, psychology, and psychoanalysis, but it will complement them. Ho'oponopono is an art of living, an evolutionary tool, not a medical treatment.

Dreams

For Freud, a dream is the fruit of your unconscious. It is the manifestation of your unconscious desires and impulses. A dream expresses what you keep hidden, either consciously or unconsciously. It is a kind of outlet or valve that makes it possible to release overly strong tensions in your unconscious in order to maintain your conscious equilibrium. The evocation of a memory during a dream generally indicates that it is time for a solution to be found. This is why dreams are another way to grasp erroneous memories buried deep within your unconscious. It is, therefore, worth doing Hoʻoponopono on memories that are unearthed during your dream life.

This is why, even if you are no longer aware of it, even if you can no longer remember it, this conflict will continue to spawn stress, anxiety, or depression. But it will also continue attracting new unpleasant situations of the same nature.

It so happens that the unconscious mind is quite powerful. The reason this is so, remember, is that all your decisions are the fruit of unconscious motivations. You think you chose this job because it was the best one available for you financially or for advancing your career? Nothing of the sort! These reasons are put forth by your conscious mind to pull the wool over your eyes. The real reason is, for example, that you chose it to please your parents and thereby attract their acknowledgment, or, to the contrary, the better to sabotage your career because an unconscious belief is telling you that you are worthless. These processes are totally unconscious. They are the result of old, unresolved conflicts, of beliefs and fears that are present in your subconscious mind and have become so many memories; in other words, programs that steer and direct you. The good memories will help your advancement (which is rarely the case in contentious situations), but the bad ones will generate new unpleasant situations.

This is how psychology perfectly explains the way your conflicts, as well as the emotions connected to them, eventually move into your unconscious—thereby becoming erroneous memories that continue to give direction to your life by directly influencing your decisions and actions.

This is why it is important to thank the disagreeable events that have come into your life, for they are showing you the existence of the erroneous memories you hold in your unconscious—and of which you are unaware—that are the guiding forces of your life without your knowledge. By revealing evidence of them, the unpleasant event allows you to ask for their removal, freeing you at the same time from their unconscious tyrannical presence. In other words, psychology demonstrates that the erroneous memories responsible for unpleasant situations in your life come from your unconscious mind. This is why you do not know you have them. These unpleasant events have to arise in order for you to become aware of their existence. All that is left for you to do is Ho'oponopono.

Epigenetics and Ho'oponopono

There is only one way to fail, and that is by giving up before you succeed.

OLIVIER LOCKERT

Conventional medicine has long thought that individual genes were acquired once and for all during conception, and remained immutable until death. Only mutations—which are produced accidentally by radiation or pollutants and most often are deleterious, if not carcinogenic—are capable of altering this genome.

But discoveries in epigenetics have compelled many to abandon this viewpoint. These discoveries show that your environment and the events that occur during the course of your life can change the expression of your genes.

In 1942 biologist, paleontologist, and geneticist Conrad Hal Waddington (1905–1975) pointed to epigenetic phenomena to explain the implications of environment on the genes and phenotype (observable characteristics) of a human being. However, we had to wait decades for epigenetics to finally enter the domain of modern research. Now it is completely revolutionizing medical thought and may lead to groundbreaking understanding about the genesis of diseases, as well as new therapeutic methods.

Observations on epigenetics have shown that "epigenetic tags" reacting to signals from the environment, such as stress, pollution[3] (including that suffered in utero[4]), poor diet,[5] periods of famine, tobacco addiction, and even in vitro fertilization[6] can alter genes. They've also shown that these changes are transmissible[7] to children and grandchildren, and are therefore hereditary.

These alterations don't change the genes, in the sense of removing one gene and replacing it with another. These changes affect only the "expression" of the genes, meaning the specific cells within the genes that are able to open or close and be modified. This is not mutation; chemical tags in the body modify the DNA and the proteins it wraps around (histones), but there is no change to the sequence of the DNA.

Over the recent past a number of enthusiastic studies have

been carried out on epigenetic phenomena regarding longevity. One study demonstrated that the lifestyle of grandparents influences the life expectancy of their grandchildren. Another study of six hundred subjects supplied evidence for a greater occurrence of epigenetic alterations than had been previously thought.[8] Approximately a third of the people in this test group presented notable genome alterations in just ten years of life.

 Epigenetics is not a marginal phenomenon but a frequent process. It may offer a good explanation of, for example, the increase in age-related illnesses, such as cancer and Alzheimer's.

Recent research established that cancer,[9] obesity,[10] type 2 diabetes,[11] allergies,[12] asthma, autism, schizophrenia, and Alzheimer's disease are at least partially attributable to epigenetic phenomena. Many more diseases are likely to be added to this far-from-exhaustive list in the future.

Another study, called GEMINAL (Gene Expression Modulation by Intervention with Nutrition and Lifestyle), which appeared in the *Proceedings of the National Academy of Sciences,* is inspiring for the possibilities it suggests.[13] This study looked at the gene evolution of men afflicted with prostate cancer, following changes in their lifestyles and independent of their treatment, whether it was conventional or not.

The researchers began by studying the genome of thirty-one volunteers who had refused all conventional treatment but were agreeable to participating in the study. They all had a Prostate Specific Antigen, or PSA rate (the blood marker for prostate cancer) lower than 10 ng/ml; and a Gleason score (indicates how aggressive a cancer is) of 6 in a range from 2 to 10 on their biopsies.

The protocol they followed for three months consisted of:

- modification of diet, which had to be low in lipids and rich in whole foods and raw vegetables;
- supplementation in soy, selenium, fish oil, and vitamins C and E;
- stress management through yoga, stretching, or relaxation for one hour a day;
- walking thirty minutes a day;
- and attendance at a support group once a week.

After this period, new tumor biopsies showed evidence of numerous positive changes in their genomes, notably the decreased regulation (reduction of expression) of certain cancerous genes that encourage the activation of androgens and cellular division. The expression of genes that are activators of growth (IGF) was also reduced. Furthermore, free PSA levels were improved among the thirty participants.

This is how a change in lifestyle habits can alter the way cancerous genes express themselves in merely three months, supplementing conventional treatments and contributing enormously to the healing of this terrible disease.

The study also confirms that mind—through stress management and the verbal expression of conflicts, both included in the protocol—can make a noticeable intervention in epigenetic processes. This notion was observed earlier by the first researchers in this field, who found that individuals' personal experiences were capable of creating changes in their DNA,[14] thus indicating that thoughts and emotions can influence the expression of genes.

This matches the 1990 experiments of Russian physicist Vladimir Popenon[15] and those performed by the HeartMath Institute of California, which are quite revolutionary. They showed that:

- DNA reacts immediately to the emotions of its former host,[16] even if that individual is several miles away. The vibrations given off by DNA increase or shrink in accordance with feelings, and neither distance nor time have any influence over this phenomenon.
- DNA structure alters in accordance with the emotions of its former host. Its helices have a tendency to relax with loving thoughts and to constrict with aggressive ones.
- The body's DNA has a direct influence on matter, and therefore on the world. This was particularly demonstrated by its effect on photons, which are light particles, which become organized in the presence of DNA and, remarkably, remain in that order even after the DNA has been removed.

DNA structure can be compared to that of a language in which the molecules function like letters of the alphabet.[17] Furthermore, it seems that it is easy to reprogram with the help of vibrations—sounds, stones, lights, radiation, and so on.

This is how your thoughts and emotions are able to change your DNA, which, through its own ability to affect matter, will change your world. The mechanics of this process offer a perfect explanation for how Ho'oponopono works: the erasure of an erroneous memory brings about a change in your thoughts and emotions, which immediately leads to changes in your DNA, which, in turn, will transform your environment by virtue of its effect on matter.

Epigenetic processes therefore allow us to better grasp and even partially explain why and how Ho'oponopono works.

The Shamanic Roots of Ho'oponopono

The new is always inside and never outside; everything is within you, not outside of you.
GITTA MALLASZ, *TALKING WITH ANGELS*

Shamanism

Shamanism has been practiced on our planet for several millennia. Some authors claim shamanism's origins are in Siberia or Central Asia, but its ubiquitous presence over the entire globe offers grounds for doubting that contention. Furthermore, shamanism was practiced widely in Europe. The majority of prehistoric caverns were once ceremonial sites where shamanic journeys were undertaken regularly. The druids, in their day, were great shamans. In Greece, Plato spoke of holy priests who used techniques that allowed them to travel outside of their bodies.

A path of oral transmission, shamanism has vanished from some parts of the world but still thrives among certain peoples, such as the Mongols, native peoples of North and South America, and aborigines of Australia.

 Shamanism is closely connected to animist thought, which sees a living presence in all elements of nature, including plants, rocks, wind, and rain. Since all of these are perceived as being endowed with life force, they are considered worthy of the highest respect.

A shaman creates a connection between the human world and that of the spirits. He journeys into the invisible realms in search of answers to questions that concern his tribe (for example, where to set up camp or where to hunt) or an individual in his community (such as illness, relational concerns, or conjugal issues).

The Origins of Ho'oponopono

Originally Ho'oponopono was a ritual used by villagers in the Hawaiian Islands to resolve community problems. All members of the tribe gathered together and shared their problems and conflicts. Once this had been done, each individual asked forgiveness for the inappropriate and even erroneous thoughts that might have been the cause of the problem.

In these earlier times, Ho'oponopono was organized by shamans in respect for the "spirits" and was also connected to the Divine. They believed that thoughts emitted and actions performed by human beings as a result of erroneous memories could also disrupt the world of the spirits, or worse, summon— or create—troublemaking spirits. Ho'oponopono was therefore used as a reconciliation technique among members of the village, but it also ensured that they remained in perfect harmony with the world around them. This allowed them to earn the good graces of the nature spirits.

Modern Ho'oponopono

Over time, this ritual became somewhat neglected. It was only in the second part of the second half of the twentieth century that the Hawaiian shaman we mentioned earlier, Morrnah Nalamaku Simeona, revised this ritual to appeal to modern tastes. She was a *kahuna lapaʻau,* priest and healer (*kahuna* meaning priest or sorcerer and *lapaʻau* meaning healer).

Morrnah explained: "We are the accumulation of all our experiences, which amounts to saying that we are burdened by our past." The memory created by each experience is stored in the form of a thought in the etheric body, which is the subtle body closest to the physical body.

Inspired by the ancient ritual, she came up with a new protocol that could be practiced alone, without the assistance of anyone else. It appealed to the divine Higher Power to heal disruptive thoughts and memories. It can therefore be best described as a process of reconciliation with yourself by virtue of love energy.

Hoʻoponopono tells us that we are the creators of all that surrounds us and that by changing our thoughts, we are able to create harmonious lives. This is not so very far from the shamanic viewpoint of the ancestral ways. In fact, the ancestors believed that the erroneous thoughts of individuals had a deleterious effect on the spirits that lived in their close proximity, and that these spirits would consequently send them unpleasant situations in return. Conversely, by thinking more positively and erasing their erroneous memories, these same individuals would restore harmonious relations with the spirits of the invisible world, who would then shower them with favors.

The Formation of the Human Being

Hoʻoponopono makes it possible to re-create the balance between the outside world (visible and invisible) and the inner world. They perceived that what we might call "self identity" is made up of four elements:

- *unihipili,* or unconscious mind, which stores the memories of past experiences and emotions;
- *uhane,* or conscious mind, which corresponds with our reason and intelligence;
- *aumalua,* or higher self (soul), which resides in a higher dimension;
- and spark, or divine intelligence, the source of inspiration and the identity of the self.

The ideal state exists when these four parts are equally balanced. It is interesting to note that contemporary medicine is of the same opinion concerning the conscious and the unconscious (but has nothing to say about the soul or divine spark), which must be in balance for the mental health of an individual.

The purpose of Ho'oponopono is to restore equilibrium between the four parts of your identity, so that you are able to reconnect with your divine spark (or inner God) and recover your inner peace. For Morrnah, peace began with the self. She said, "We are only here to bring peace into our lives, and if we bring peace into our lives, everything around us will finds its proper place, rhythm, and peace."

According to the shamanic vision, Ho'oponopono makes it possible to recover our inner and outer equilibrium, and restore balance within ourselves and with the spirits of nature.

 Human beings are weighed down by their past. When they are feeling stress or fear, they should look within themselves. They will then see that the cause of their discomfort is one of their memories. To eliminate their stress or fear, all they need to do is erase it.

The Cathars

The Cathar religion developed rapidly in southern France from the tenth to fourteenth centuries, most notably in the Languedoc region, due primarily to the striking beauty and simplicity of its precepts, especially in comparison to those of the Christian church of that time.[18] The true Cathars did not live in castles but in caves or huts, thanks to the gifts of local inhabitants whose labors they shared.

The Cathar religion was ahead of its time. It spoke of a unique, good God and the teachings of Jesus Christ. Its doctrine was similar to that of early Christians before the institution of official dogmas, which altered basic meanings. The Cathars preached humility, compassion, and love. They believed that every individual was capable of forming a direct personal relationship with God, with no religious clergy needed as intermediary.

The *perfecti*—men and women enjoying equal status—formed the priesthood of this religion. They lived an ascetic lifestyle and concentrated on spreading the good word throughout the countryside. They hoped through this work to be able to leave the cycle of reincarnations so they could remain in the other world—the world of God—in the form of entities who were mind-soul-body beings of light.

The training of perfecti was a long one. It required a harsh initiation that put them in touch with themselves but also with the spirits of nature, with whom they communicated and for whom they held the highest respect. This makes them akin to great shamans. They were also heirs to the ancient mystery schools.

Cathar doctrine indicates that the tangible world is propped up by a preexisting world of the spirit. Contrary to what is sometimes said in a very simplistic way, the Cathars did not consider the physical world as evil and the spiritual world as good. They saw in matter an imperfect but necessary world in which individuals could gradually purify themselves, one incarnation after another, and acquire knowledge of their imperfections. Some proponents of dualism will say that "good" needs "evil" for individuals to progress, which is more or less true. But, in fact, the only thing that counts is the evolution of beings.

Whatever the case may be, Cathar philosophy is not far from the vision of Ho'oponopono in some aspects. In fact, matter and the world that surrounds you reveals your imperfections to you; it is up to you to eliminate the erroneous thoughts attached to you, so that you can purify yourself more and more, and thereby reach the world of the spirit and harmony.

The Realization of Thoughts

The thought is only a flash in the middle of the night. But this flash is everything.

HENRI POINCARÉ, *THE VALUE OF SCIENCE*

In every moment your mind is manufacturing a considerable number and variety of thoughts that are not always very well organized. Most of them are produced by your mind, which never stops chattering about everything and nothing, constantly commenting and forming judgments about you and other people.

These thoughts are pieces of information focused on energies; in other words, they are embryonic "entities" with a life of their own and the sole desire to live and evolve. They are projected into the future and will energetically create potential future events.

 The present is only the consequence of past thoughts.

You are today what you were thinking yesterday. You become what you think.

You are surrounded by the future that your thoughts created. Your present is only the realization of one among all of them.

Most fortunately, your many contradictory thoughts— "I am great"; "I am nobody"—mutually lessen their effect by virtue of the relationship between opposing forces. However, these thoughts—these potential futures—will do everything they can to develop and manifest.

To do this, the same thoughts will have a tendency to often pop up in your mind so they can feed on your psychic energy and keep growing, and thereby become stronger and stronger. Fixed notions and obsessions are excellent examples of these kinds of thoughts, especially when you imagine that you are poor and a loser. This thought will continue to develop in your energy and among your potential futures until it becomes your reality, which will further confirm this feeling: "I knew it." This will in turn create new situations that encourage feelings of being worthless. In short, it is a vicious cycle.

Knowing this, it is important to instead visualize that you are intelligent, enjoying good health, and have great success in life. This, of course, corresponds to the positive thinking of Emile Coué, a French psychologist and pharmacist in the early twentieth century who devised an auto-suggestion method using positive thinking; the visualization technique of American oncologist and author Dr. Carl Simonton; and the law of attraction.

Your thoughts attract situations that will confirm them. If you think you are worthless, a large number of things will happen in your everyday life that reinforce your belief in this notion. If you believe that life is dangerous, numerous situations will arise offering confirmation of this feeling (accidents, incidents, severe weather, epidemics). You created this vision of the world, and the world has simply complied with your expectations by becoming dangerous for you.

Your thoughts will be amplified by similar thoughts and situations that resonate with them; this is how they both feed and confirm them. All this will push you to take them more and more seriously, and more importantly, take them for reality, which will ensure that your thoughts will be able to manifest themselves fully realized. They are going to become your reality in the present. This forms a veritable vicious circle that grows larger with time; it has a snowball effect. Eventually it will become almost impossible for you to realize that what you are living is not reality but simply the world you have invented.

 Erroneous thoughts will cause poor potential futures and thereby situations that will be painful to live through in the present, whereas good thoughts will bring harmony and love into your life.

Your environment is made up of many potentials waiting to manifest if the opportunity is given to them; in other words, if your thoughts summon them.

This is why it is important in the first place to monitor your thoughts. Meditation is a great technique for this. It allows you to quiet your mind and see what is truly essential for you. But if, despite your best efforts, a negative thought escapes your vigilance—"I am a loser"—then send right afterward the opposite thought—"I am capable"—to annihilate the first.

Ho'oponopono makes it possible to eliminate bad potential futures that could materialize by erasing the erroneous memory that generated them. It can offer a great deal of assistance in this regard.

Dreamtime

Dreamtime is an important element in Australian aboriginal culture. Its importance lies in the fact that it corresponds to the immaterial period that preceded and anticipated the creation of the world. It is also the place we all go after death.

Australian aborigines believe that everything that materializes has already been thought and constructed energetically before it manifests in our world. Conversely, everything that manifests is the consequence of a thought that has been shaped by memories.

Ho'oponopono Explained
by Quantum Physics

One grows weary of everything except
understanding.

VIRGIL

We all learned in school about Newtonian physics—that apples fall vertically from above to below, by virtue of gravity. However, while this lesson was still being taught to us, discoveries in quantum physics were already showing that this vision of the world is limited and not exactly true.

Quantum Physics

Quantum physics appears extremely complicated when you look at the mathematical formulas used for demonstrations. This has prompted some people to ask what possessed God to create such a complicated universe. But if the demonstrations are difficult for most people to grasp, the answers they obtain are quite simple—relatively speaking—and clear. They are therefore within the reach of everyone.

 One of the first lessons quantum physics teaches is that matter, as we customarily conceive of it, does not exist.

In truth, far from the physical appearance we imagine, matter is nothing but a gigantic concentration of energy. Each particle of the universe is only concentrated energy. The particles combine to form atoms, then the molecules that are the origin of visible matter. This is why we can say that matter is comprised entirely of energy.

The universe is formed by countless particles separated by immense empty spaces. In other words, matter consists mostly of emptiness. But then, what gives it its appearance of solidity? Binding forces connect the particles and can also be found among the planets of the solar system and the galaxies. There are weak interactions, strong interactions, gravitational forces, and electromagnetic forces.

More disturbing is the fact that this matter can give back energy, then reassemble new particles (matter) in a vast movement of destruction and creation called wave-corpuscle duality. It is like water transforming into steam before returning to a fluid state when the temperature lowers. This means that energy and matter are only two aspects of the same element, and the universe is constantly making and unmaking itself.

To organize energy and matter requires the presence of information; otherwise the energy will remain formless. Matter was not produced first, then spirit, and finally consciousness. American astrophysicist and cosmologist George Fitzgerald Smoot, a 2006 Nobel Prize winner, said that photos of the birth of the universe taken by the COBE (1989 Cosmic Background Explorer) satellite would reveal the "face of God." Popular science writers Igor and Grichka Bogdanov discuss in their disputed book *Le visage de Dieu* (The face of God) the hypothesis shared by numerous scientists—including Smoot—of a kind of cosmic DNA; in other words, the presence of cosmic information that would have given order to the general direction taken by the universe from the time of the Big Bang.

Information is, therefore, essential for the appearance and functioning of the universe. It is transported by energy, like radio waves. Today we know that there are "nonlinear waves" capable of traveling across the entire universe without diminishing in strength, and at speeds far greater than that of light. It is therefore very easy for information to travel from one end of the universe to the other. What information does is "inform," or give form to matter. Conversely, all forms contain some piece of information.

But according to astrophysicists, some 96 percent of the universe is "missing," which is quite a large part.[19] They call this vast portion "dark matter" (73 percent) and "dark energy" (23 percent)—and so far nobody understands this "missing" piece. This dark matter is omnipresent, similar to what the ancients called ether. Swiss-born scientist Nassim Haramein believes this missing matter is simply the energy of the void, meaning we are immersed in an ocean of energy that fills all the spaces between particles and among planets and galaxies. This would be describable as random energy (incoherent), whereas matter, in his opinion, would be characterized as organized energy (coherent). Coherence (materialization) is given energy by information.

The energy of the void could be the next source of energy for humanity. This is what is often called "free energy," which would be at the disposal of everyone and completely free, as the American engineer Nikola Tesla (1856–1943) envisioned it almost a century ago.

Energy Man

The human being, as a part of the universe, is comprised of the same elements as the universe is: matter/energy and information. Only the names for these elements have changed. We talk of the physical body, energy circulation, and mind/thought. This means that, constitutionally, the human being is first and foremost comprised of energy, like the universe, even before being chemical and biological.

On the physiological level, the work of Russian researcher Georges Lakhovsky (1869–1942), author of *L'origine de la vie*, showed that every cell of the body is an oscillating minicircuit that emits and absorbs electromagnetic waves at precise frequencies. It was later discovered that cells communicate to each other and with their environment by releasing light (photons).

DNA is even more amazing. In fact, DNA is nothing but pure information. It is the actual transmitter/receiver of the cell that puts it in constant contact with its environment, both immediate and remote—in other words, with the quantum world surrounding it. It is also capable of acting on matter, as we saw earlier in our discussion of epigenetics.

Thought

The DNA experiments we looked at earlier led to researchers taking greater interest in the effect of thought on matter, and therefore on the environment. There is a large body of evidence that shows the influence of human thought on the body. For example, we could cite the placebo effect, the positive thinking and visualization techniques cited earlier, hypnosis, sophrology, and so forth. All of these offer proof that your thoughts act directly and constantly on your body.

The power of thought goes far beyond what we customarily imagine, as Dr. Deepak Chopra observed.[20] Chopra wrote about the psychiatric disorder in which multiple personalities express themselves in the same individual. Studies showed that an individual with this disorder was capable of being diabetic (insulin dependent), epileptic, color blind, having high blood pressure or allergies, and even exhibiting scars, warts, or skin rashes, depending on which personality was dominant. Furthermore, the transition from one personality to another could happen with lightning speed. Chopra observed that each personality altered the biology of its host body just as quickly. His conclusion was that if psychotic individuals are capable of this, everyone possesses the ability to transform personal biology with the power of the mind.

The thoughts of others can also influence you without your awareness. Author Masaru Emoto reported experiments showing that thought can affect the structural formation of ice crystals, depending on what type of thoughts have been transmitted to the water.[21] This would indicate that thoughts—your own or others'—can alter the structure of the water present in your body. It is common knowledge that the bodies of human beings are 60–75 percent water, so based on Emoto's research, that is a high percentage subject to disruptive thoughts, especially when they are negative in your regard.

Prayer

Prayer draws on thought in vibrations of help, love, and compassion; in other words, the highest human vibrations. It also draws on other subtle energies present in the universe.

A study reported by Dr. Larry Dossey at New York's Columbia University in 2001 showed that prayers performed by groups drawn from many religions in Canada, Australia, and the United States improved in vitro fertilization results for Korean women who had been treated for sterility.[22] The pregnancy rate went from 26 percent in the control group to 50 percent in those who had prayers said for them, although the beneficiaries were unaware that these groups were praying on their behalf.

The Harris (et al.) study carried out in the United States in 1990 obtained similar results on 990 individuals hospitalized in a coronary care unit in Kansas City.[23] Those who had been the beneficiaries of prayers reported 10 percent fewer postoperative complications than the others. Similarly, Professor Herbert Benson of Harvard University believes that patients who repeatedly pray are capable of triggering changes in their own organ function.[24]

Praying for yourself or for other people could therefore offer another possible method for getting rid of some erroneous memories. However, while the results are obvious, it will not be relevant to all individuals, whereas with Ho'oponopono—taking full responsibility for the situation and requesting the elimination of the erroneous memory connected with it—the effects seem more reliable and arrive more quickly.

Another study showed that happiness is contagious.[25] A twenty-year study done on 4,739 people between the years 1983 and 2003 showed that an emotion like happiness can be transmitted to your associates, present or not. Groups of happy and unhappy people were identified among the test subjects. The study's authors were then able to observe that happiness spread to the third degree of separation (into the friends of friends). They even established that if a person had a friend living within a mile radius who was happy, it increased their probability of experiencing feelings of happiness by 25 percent. Similar results were observed between spouses, brothers and sisters, and even close neighbors. Happiness can truly be described as contagious. However, this effect has a tendency to diminish over time and distance.

All this clearly shows that your thoughts act on your body and also affect your morale and that of others. In fact, the effects of your thoughts go even further, as demonstrated by Vladimir Popenon's experiment cited earlier, which explains how emotions are capable of having an effect on matter.

According to Gregg Braden, author of *The Spontaneous Healing of Belief* and *Fractal Time,* this effect of thought would also have been observed on the earth's magnetic field following the World Trade Center attack of September 11, 2001. These events triggered such profound trauma in the minds of countless individuals that Braden believes the mass of mental energy released at that moment could have altered the electromagnetism of the earth.

Soviet aerodynamics professor and engineer Marina Popovitch, a retired record-holding test pilot, believes there is a permanent interaction between human emotions and the earth's electromagnetic field. In support of her contention, Russian researchers have observed the presence of dark zones in this field when wars are raging. Popovitch also maintains that the thoughts emitted by humanity can affect solar activity. She believes our planet has reached a saturation point and is reacting to this excess with violent disturbances—earthquakes, eruptions, floods, and so on.

At some future time when these findings can be confirmed, and when the principle behind them has been extrapolated, it probably will reveal that the influence of the human mind extends even further. This is because nonlinear waves can travel to the ends of the universe without being diminished. The fluttering of a butterfly's wings in Tokyo is capable of triggering an aurora borealis on a planet in another galaxy far, far away. What else might be possible?

Our environment is made up entirely of energy and informed matter. Thought can influence it on both an individual and a planetary scale, on both the microscopic and macroscopic planes.

 Ho'oponopono makes it possible to change these thoughts (pieces of information) by erasing the negative memories that interact and shape your surrounding material environment. Once the negative thoughts have been erased, positive thoughts will be able to develop at leisure and generate a balanced equilibrium.

It is easy now to see, thanks to quantum physics, why this process of reconciling with yourself is capable of bringing harmony into your mind, body, and world.

Is Our World Real?

We are what we think.

BUDDHA

After reading the preceding paragraphs you might be legitimately wondering whether the world in which you are living is truly real or you might just be dreaming it. Because if everything is only information and energy, and you are the creator of 100 percent of your life by virtue of your thought alone, then you can rightly ask yourself if the universe as you regularly imagine it might not simply be the fruit of your thoughts.

This notion seems pertinent because there are several elements that tend to give the impression you are living in a dream.

The Brain

First, you should know that your subconscious mind does not distinguish between real and imaginary, nor between action and thought. MRIs (Magnetic Resonance Imaging) of brain function reveal that the same zones of your brain are activated whether performing an action or watching someone else perform that action, or even when imagining performing that action. So you can ask yourself if you are really performing an action or if you are simply imagining that you are taking action.

This inability of our brain to distinguish real from imaginary has made it possible to develop certain symbolic therapies that are able to give relief to people for some of their conflicts. For example, if you still have a disagreement with a dead person, it's obviously impossible to talk it out with the dead person. But you can still find relief for your pain by writing a letter to the person and perhaps even mailing it. Your brain will then regard this action as if it had actually been performed and the deceased individual had actually received this message, which will relieve much of your tension generated by the unresolved grievance.

When you realize this, you will understand that it is easy to trick your brain and make it take an illusion for reality. In the same way, you can just as thoroughly fool yourself and believe that the life you are living is a reality when it is, in fact, nothing but an illusion.

The Human Being

Like the universe, the human being is made up of matter/energy on the one hand and information/thoughts on the other, as we discussed earlier. But if we really think about it, just what is it that defines a human being? It is neither matter nor the physical body, but thoughts. This viewpoint reportedly led physicist Jacqueline Bousquet[26] to say, "The human being is, in fact, only a handful of memories," which directly agrees with the contention of Ho'oponopono that erroneous memories need to be eliminated.

Thought releases energetic waves that can be measured scientifically, as shown by the electroencephalograms used in medicine. Furthermore, we have seen that thought is capable of acting on matter. This phenomenon has caused quantum researchers a great deal of discomfort. From their earliest research they perceived that their thoughts, in other words, their expectations, had a transformative effect on the experiments they were performing. If they were expecting a result in the domain of vibrations, than a result from this domain was precisely what they got. If another researcher performing an identical experiment was hoping for an answer relating to blood cells, this is what was obtained. This phenomenon was called "the observer effect on subparticles."

But in addition to altering the surrounding world, thought is also capable of *creating* it, which is a much more powerful state of affairs, I am sure you will agree. This is first manifested in the energetic universe and then materialized in the physical universe, if the thoughts are transmitted with sufficient conviction. This is how your thoughts, influenced by your memories, build the world in which you live. The responsibility for constructing this environment is yours, and it was made visible by virtue of the thoughts you produced. But does the world really exist or is it simply something from the domain of dreams?

Awareness of the Surrounding World

This naturally leads to the question of knowing how you know the world that surrounds you. In fact, you grasp it solely through your five senses. Your vision of the outside world is a depiction manufactured in your brain out of information from your five senses. You believe in the existence of objects because you see them, touch them, feel them, and hear them through your sense organs. However, your perceptions are only thoughts in your mind, and your brain is locked inside a box that is completely isolated from the world surrounding it.

Your five senses operate in a vibratory mode and in no way on a material/physical level, as you may be tempted to think. We have long known this is true for sounds and colors, and now we know it is true for scents[27] as well, which are also vibratory by nature and nonmolecular. We know this because molecules that are quite similar in chemical structure are capable of producing totally different odors. The sole explanation for this difference is that the sense of smell operates on a vibratory not a chemical level. It is very likely that touch works in the same way. As matter is formed of concentrated waves, it is hard to imagine that it might be otherwise.

This is how your knowledge of your environment is solely vibratory. This explains why it is so easily shaped by your thoughts, beliefs, fears, and values, which act as filters altering your perception of the universe that surrounds you.

Furthermore, your senses capture only a part of your ambient information. Humans are unable to detect all the sounds, colors, and odors. Some animals have a much more extensive range than humans—ultrasounds or infrared, for example. Therefore, the reality you perceive is quite fragmentary. What this means is that the part of the universe that is visible to your senses is quite tiny relative to all the waves being produced in your environment.

Finally, we need to remember that the information captured by the five senses is coded by electrical impulses before the nerves transmit it to the brain. The brain then reconstructs the surrounding universe out of the information it has received using blueprints provided by your system of thought. This image of the world is therefore truncated by the way it is captured, its mode of transmission, the brain's abilities to reconstruct it, and finally, by your psychological filters that seek by any and all means to ensure that the received image is placed in your system of reference. Despite all this, it is this image that is reality for you. However, this reality is not located outside of you but deep inside your head. All of this exists only in your mind. In other words, you can be greatly deceived by illusions when you imagine that the universe, just like everything surrounding you, has an existence outside your mind.

You could very easily believe that this reality was created from whole cloth by your brain, or else that the information it receives is not real and is only the fruit of your imagination, or more precisely, manipulations that were sent by you. You have no proof that the outside world really exists. This is what makes it possible to think that reality does not exist and you are simply living a dream. During a dream you also see things, touch things, hear things, and feel things as you do in reality. Wherein lies the difference? What makes you believe that what you experience during the day is real life and the images that come while you are sleeping are only dreams? It is only your thoughts and prejudices that give you this impression.

Your entire organism could be only an image, an illusion like the universe that surrounds you; even your brain could be an illusion. The human being would, thereby, have no reality. Your experiences would be deceptive and the whole universe nothing but an illusion. *All that would remain of you would be thought.* The human being would therefore be nothing but a set of thoughts, which is to say, a set of memories that act upon an illusory reality.

 You are only the imagination of yourself.

In a very near future, computers will be capable of transmitting to your brain virtual information that is visual, auditory, olfactory, gustatory, and tactile in nature, which will give you the impression that you are living in a real world, whereas this world would be formed by the computer. You will also be able to send it information/thoughts and thereby converse with it, obtain changes from it to the information it sends you, and thus prompt changes in the imaginary world that it has created with you in mind, and which you take for reality.

It is exactly the same in your present reality: you can act on events with your thoughts. By changing your thought, you are changing the dream you are experiencing—your everyday reality—with childlike ease, perhaps without even realizing you have changed it.

The Quantum Aspect

Just a century ago, the image we held of the world was one of a tangible, material, measurable world (Newtonian physics). Then quantum physics appeared on the scene and everything got turned around to such an extent that today our environment has become largely virtual, made up solely of energy and information. Our vision of the world has gone from reality to abstraction. The universe itself would be born of a "singularity" in which matter and energy would come from something that remains undefined and would have no boundaries in time or space. This is presumably what prompted Jacqueline Bousquet to say: "The universe behaves more like a thought than like a mechanism."

The universe would be like a thought in this respect. The idea is beautiful and poetic. It cannot help but bring to mind certain mythological texts. What now remains to be determined is the identity of what produced this thought. Of course, the notion of a great architect who organized this is very seductive. As we have seen, some astrophysicists speak of cosmic DNA to indicate the probable presence of an overarching information manager in the cosmos. But they do not make clear where this DNA comes from, nor who, in fact, created it.

In fact, it could be much simpler than that. Being the sole creator of everything that takes place in your life, you could be in the process of creating in each instant the environment in which you have evolved. As noted by astrophysicist Hubert Reeves, "Matter will form only under your gaze." This phrase perfectly sums up a long list of research studies in quantum physics. It means that matter will only inform itself—take shape—when you are looking at it. It should be specified that in this case the word *gaze* should be understood as meaning "thought." It is your thought that gives consistency to energy and therefore transforms it into matter. Otherwise it remains in its random energetic form. This is how *your* thought creates *all* matter and the *entire* universe that surrounds you.

There is no such thing as chance or coincidence or synchronicity or providence . . . there is nothing but you sending messages to yourself.

Your unconscious is constantly sending messages to your conscious mind through the intermediary of the accidents and coincidences it creates in your universe. This is because it is capable of creating everything in your environment, even the most incredible things: apparitions, earthquakes, climatic changes, revolution, encounters, luck, chance, and so on. Everything is possible for it, simply because it is its world; because it is your world.

Your attention created the universe before your eyes, following the thoughts that you are constantly producing and those you produced (realization of thoughts on a material level) in the past. It is therefore simple to grasp how by changing your thoughts—as is the case by virtue of Ho'oponopono, in which you erase your erroneous memories—you change the construction of the universe, which is to say your construction of your self.

This creation is carried out immediately and unconsciously. But the problem is that it is the unconscious that is directing your mind with its good and bad memories. This is why the elimination of erroneous memories is very important, because it makes it possible to gradually harmonize the world in which you are living.

Do Other People Exist?

If the environment is the fruit of your creation, a question arises: Do other individuals really exist? When asked about this, Dr. Len answered: "Others? What others?" I think this is a joke intended to make it easy to really grasp Ho'oponopono. Because other people do exist, in fact, as their own individuals. However, they respond completely to your creation, otherwise they would not be present in "your" world.

It must be understood that there is not one world—planet Earth—on which seven billion individuals are living, but to the contrary, there are seven billion worlds united by a common consciousness. These worlds are linked together by a framework and must obey the laws inherent in this environment (space/time). The material world serves as this framework, which is to say it serves as a kind of mutual support in which all human beings develop their own personal worlds.

It is possible—even quite probable, according to physicists—that many universes exist that are parallel to our own, in which every individual explores other potential futures. In other words, we lead different lives in these other universe that permit different enriching experiences for personal development. In other words, they posit, we live in several universes at a time, in which we coexist and develop different experiences.

All this goes to show that it is not at all certain the universe really exists in the sense that we customarily think it does. Quantum physics even seems to offer proof of the exact opposite. In this case, it is easy to understand that your thoughts determine the illusion you are living, or rather the one you think you are living. By erasing deleterious thoughts, Ho'oponopono allows you to live a harmonious life in which you can achieve your deepest aspirations.

The Consequences of Ho'oponopono for Individuals

They did not know it was impossible, so they did it.

MARK TWAIN

The first perceptible element of Ho'oponopono is that it offers you relief during the difficult times of your life. With it, there is no need to analyze situations or pursue extensive research. By erasing disruptive memories, Ho'oponopono puts an end to an unpleasant situation so that it can steer you into more quiet waters.

However, Ho'oponopono is an art of living and not a therapy. It will never replace a psychiatric consultation or any form of psychotherapy. It will, on the other hand, supplement them harmoniously and provide relief for the majority of minor daily conflicts. It is therefore advisable to perform it whenever anything disagreeable occurs in your life. But it should be clearly understood that in the event of a serious disorder or if the problem persists, it is imperative to consult a doctor or other professional.

You cannot know where the elimination of a memory with Ho'oponopono will lead. You simply know that it will allow you to improve your present situation by extricating you from a difficult situation. This is how any problem that crops up in your life can be settled simply through working solely on yourself.

Then, over the course of time as you discard your erroneous memories, you will begin to truly discover yourself, who you really are, what you really want in the depths of your soul, and what your essential aspirations are. You will little by little glimpse your true identity. This will, of course, change the way you think, and thereby your world will become more harmonious and fully assimilated in your deepest desires. You can then develop your talents and explore numerous potential futures that will be propitious for your personal evolution.

The elimination of erroneous thoughts will allow you to recover your wholeness, which is extremely important for encouraging new energies. You will consciously become the creator of your world and no longer have to suffer it unconsciously and randomly, as is now the case. You will then be the true master of your fate.

Ho'oponopono and New Energies

There is no path to happiness. Happiness is the path.
TRADITIONAL SAYING

We have seen that we live in seven billion worlds that are all connected by a common consciousness. This consciousness forms the framework that links together all the worlds we create for ourselves. These universes are entirely autonomous and depend solely on the thoughts of their owners. However, they must answer for certain rules connected to the space/time in which we are evolving. As it happens, there are two phenomena currently occurring in our planetary environment.

- The electromagnetic field of the earth is expanding. This has been observed on the level of the Schumann resonance.* This increase in size is the result of a more

---

*The ionosphere possesses resonance capacities that were discovered by the German physicist W. O. Schumann. Schumann resonances are a set of spectral peaks in the extremely low frequency area (3 to 30 Hz) of the terrestrial electromagnetic field.

general increase that is affecting, at the least, our entire galaxy. The cause is the arrival of new cosmic energies that give human beings heightened awareness, new visions, new abilities, and new thoughts. But before they can make use of the expansion of their awareness and abilities, humans need to adapt to them, a process that requires time, calm, and discernment. This is the transitional period we are now actually crossing through. This period of adaptation is expressed by fatigue, irritability, anxiety, and depression.

• As mentioned earlier, the thoughts produced by human beings interfere with the earth's electromagnetic field. It is currently saturated because of the many disruptive events humanity has produced: wars, famines, murders, injustice, tension, crises, revolutions, and so on. It is so saturated with these discordant events that the planet is reacting violently with earthquakes, volcanic eruptions, floods, and other natural disasters, which only intensify the saturation process. Such catastrophes are making this transitional period even more difficult.

To get through this delicate phase, it is important for each person to lighten his or her load as much as possible. On the physical plane, a life in balance is essential, of course, with an organic diet, plenty of exercise and other physical activities, relaxation, and so forth. On the mental plane, we need to find solutions to old conflicts and erase all our old limiting values and beliefs, as well as our fears. All of this must be carried out quite quickly, because energies are evolving at an extremely rapid pace right now. This is why techniques such as psychotherapy, psychoanalysis, NLP (Neuro-Linguistic

Programming), and EMDR,* which provide a lot of help in pathological cases, are hardly useful here, as they are too weighty (they require a therapist) and too slow.

Fortunately, new and easy-to-use tools have been developed—as if by chance—that are quick, effective, and can be employed personally. These include two acupressure-related techniques, EFT (Emotional Freedom Technique) and TAT (Tapas Acupressure Technique), as well as Zensight† meditation, temporal openness,‡ energetic treatments,§ and of course, Ho'oponopono.

> Among all these tools, Ho'oponopono is without contest the most effective for the period we are now going through, because it allows you to rapidly discard all erroneous memories and thus adapt more easily to new energies that will guide you to a higher state of consciousness.

Today, with events occurring at a faster and faster pace, it is not always necessary to perform the entire protocol, "Sorry, forgive me, thank you, I love you," to get results. It is often enough to simply ask that whatever erroneous memory is connected with this or that event you are experiencing be erased. This technique evolves over time and becomes increasingly faster and more effective.

---

*EMDR, or Eye Movement Desensitization and Reprocessing, is a technique frequently used in treating PTSD (posttraumatic stress disorder).

† For more information, go to www.sophiemerle.com.

‡ Developed by physicist Jean-Pierre Garnier Malet. For more information, see his book *Changez votre future par les ouvertures temporelles* (Le Temps Présent, 2006).

§ Premium energetic treatments are taught by Dr. Luc Bodin and presented in workshops.

However, it would be a mistake to think you can dispose of the dark side within you in order to get through the current transitional period with no problem. To the contrary, Ho'oponopono can help you accept this dark aspect of your nature so that through it you can restore your wholeness. By taking this path, you will witness the disappearance of duality. There will no longer be any "good" or "evil"; there will simply be all. You will then see that your portion of darkness, the one you reject with such determination, is not as negative as you wish to believe. Quite the contrary, it is capable of bringing you a sense of fullness and balance that has long been absent from your life.

Thanks to the new energies of the imminent future, human beings are going to discover that they can be their own leaders and that governments, religions, directors, chiefs, gurus, and so on are no longer helpful. Human beings will become aware of their immense capabilities and develop new ones, such as telepathy, strengthened thought, and the feeling of belonging to a cosmic community. Society will find itself completely transformed because of this. It is going to become more humane and more attentive to the development of every individual while fully respecting each one's differences, uniqueness, and aspirations.[28]

Ho'oponopono is an essential element during this time of transition. By eliminating your erroneous memories, it will shed a strong light on your mind that will remove blockages and negative thoughts that induce you to believe this promising future is not possible, or at least not possible for you.

 Say "thank you" to Ho'oponopono for being there to help you find fulfillment and change the world—your world.

3

From Spirituality to Abundance

Nathalie Bodin Lamboy

Practice wanting for others what you want for yourself by being Christlike rather than a Christian, Muhammed-like rather than a Muslim, and Buddha-like rather than a Buddhist.

WAYNE DYER, *THE POWER OF INTENTION*

Spirituality Is Your Religion

Reading *spirituality* and *religion* in the same title may cause your arm to shake involuntarily, forcing you to drop the book to the ground. This is a risk I am happy to take, even if it means you might skip reading a chapter that I took pleasure in writing.

For many of you, religion has clearly lost its appeal. Whether due to intolerance, extreme behavior, or power grabs, it seems that traditional religions embody the spiritual life less and less. However, it is really thanks to the different religions that this notion of spirituality has been kept alive so long, and with it humanity's most distinctive feature.

Can we look at the holy books as a gateway to spirituality and the human beings that contributed to making them as simple messengers? Priests and monks, nuns and pastors, mothers and sages are all just like you—human beings creating their own lives on this earth. And you know as well as I that it is not easy to live in accordance with your principles every single day.

I would like to point out that I was raised among rationalists who say that only science can save the world. It was drilled into my mind that only microscopes and chemical products are life's friends. Thanks to my discriminating intelligence, I observed that facts did not always support this theory.

Over the course of years, thanks to people I met and books I read, I was able to discover religions and their adepts. Despite initially having classified gods under the heading of myths and fairy tales, as my professors had taught me, the truths at the heart of religion emerged a little more clearly every time I found the texts I read to be accurate and pertinent. This is why my view of religion is a bit singular; it is the perspective of an explorer of spirituality.

Some people say it is the fault of religion that people have gone astray, as it places all the good and bad things we experience in this world in the hands of an all-powerful God. This is how the notion that you and I are nothing but marionettes subject to fate was established. In this thought system, you are unable to do anything but simply pray that nothing falls on your head. However, this theory overlooks one important detail: free will. Nothing on this earth is immutable; everything can change once you have decided to make a change. You always have a choice.

I personally find it extremely relaxing to know that I have something to say on the matter. Furthermore, when I discovered that the sole constant in the universe is actually not that constant, I took a deep breath, knowing that the wheel is turning and happiness would one day cross my path. The religious texts brought me some good news.

Because Jesus was allegedly crucified on the cross to save us, religious practitioners might deem sacrifice the best means to atone for both your own sins and those of others. Why not?

And what if this man who suffered until he died with his arms outstretched and his heart exposed represents that part of yourself you have been careful to camouflage? You see in this flayed Christ the "deep self," as I call it, that unconscious part of yourself that beats to the same rhythm as your heart and was tortured on the altar of materiality. It is simply waiting for you to free it.

This deep self is, like Christ, in each of us, ready to spring forth, and he knows that love alone can save us. The only suffering he engenders is to make us feel there is something greater than ownership of a car and a house, and having a family. This pain is the inexpression of our spirituality.

The Bible tells of Christ's resurrection, which I consider to be a very positive sign. This deep self, this Christ crucified by fears, has come back to life. Can't you see this as an example of your ability to be the miracle in your own life? You are able to let something you hold in your deepest depths come back to life, and the best tool for doing this is love.

When I look at the cross of Jesus I tell myself that, one day, I will totally liberate this aptitude in myself, this aptitude to love everything that exists unconditionally, which will make the suffering of this cross vanish forever from my life. Imagine if all human beings made a decision to let their divine voices speak. Whether they are Catholic, Protestant, Muslim, Hindu, or whatever, as if the religion matters in this regard. At this very moment, another symbol could appear in the temples and churches, and why couldn't it be a text that says, "Thank you, I love you"?

We can always dream.

Ho'oponopono, Reincarnation, and Family

To those who share my belief in reincarnation, I would like to say that I found in the practice of Ho'oponopono a meaning in the presence of every individual in this life. I am going to summarize the principle of reincarnation as I see it, to make it easier to share my reasoning with you.

Everything begins in the notion of self, which I refer to as the deep self. This self should not be envisioned as a flesh-and-blood individual, but rather as a "traveling soul" whose apprenticeship takes place in several terrestrial lives. When you are in that state that precedes your arrival on earth, which is to say a soul, you have a global vision of the universe and the place you have to take in it. Its comprehension, it absolute knowledge, to be more exact, is gained, it seems, through the experimentation of life. And what could be better than to come to this small blue planet to pursue your education? It is at this moment that you make your choice to incarnate in a particular place as a member of a particular family. This decision seems to be forgotten once you have incarnated here but will reappear on the day you become aware that you can establish contact with your deep self—the self you set aside that will reconnect you to your adventurous soul. Perhaps you set it aside the better to find it later. This contact takes place either through meditation or by a return to nature. You feel in your very depths that you have come here to enrich your knowledge through experiences, and with a little luck, this life could be the last one you spend here—before the great leap toward nirvana.

In the meantime, you must live with the family you have chosen. An absent or violent father, a humiliating or indifferent mother, an odious or simple-minded brother, an annoying or crazy sister; they are not simply your family, it was your choice to spend an entire lifetime with them. And how will you invite compassion to enter your heart and accept this improbable choice you made by being born into such a violent or indifferent family? This invitation can only be extended by forgiving your soul, your deep self, for having decided to live among these individuals. It is simply a matter of thanking it for having made this choice. There is nothing like lovingly forgiving yourself to make it possible to next forgive others and thereby become compassionate.

The main class of the school of life is the family. It is a course you can never escape, for even as an orphan, you will be learning all its lessons from its absence.

In this concept of a reincarnation that was chosen intentionally, the family is much more than a reflection of your personality; it is the mirror of your soul. Furthermore, it is the messenger and guardian of what you are going to learn on earth.

For some it will be an apprenticeship in emotional detachment; for others it will be lessons in learning to live without expectations. The number of lives you have to live does not matter; it will be just the right amount of time necessary for your comprehension.

When I became fully aware that my choice of a family had been guided this way, I realized that I had to stop fighting my family members and stop fighting against myself. The grievances, resentments, disappointments, and expectations that I had collected against my parents and sibling gradually lost all substance. I could finally admit to myself that to have incarnated among these people had allowed me to understand so many things that it would have been impossible to find any better place to evolve. By using such simple words as "Thank you, I love you" when facing the difficulties I encountered with my family, I fully felt this gratitude. It was directed toward my father, my mother, my brother, and also toward myself. I believe that I did a bit more than simply accept my choice to be born in this family; I even learned to love the part of me that had made this choice. I began to love myself.

The practice of Ho'oponopono is a means of accelerating the process of accepting your human condition so that you can next pursue the learning process necessary for your soul or deep self to evolve.

By reincarnating here, at this time, I was seeking to participate in this discovery of love of self, or better yet, I perhaps desired to live it fully so as to attain the ultimate stage of the soul's evolution. In fact, what difference does the reason make if I feel good when practicing Ho'oponopono and accept my life here with my family? Who could ask for anything more than simply continuing this way?

You have been granted this opportunity to love, thanks to those close to you. Whether or not you believe in reincarnation, your family is there to teach you to love the part of yourself that you despise so much. It is the reflection of what you are trying to hide deep inside. It is a messenger from your deep self.

Haven't you noticed how the reflections of those close to you always sting you where it hurts most? Perhaps it is because they know you well, or more probably because you created with them the situation that brought on this conflict. You are the creator of this situation. You have put everything in place that was necessary to make these memories—which had been nesting peacefully inside—reveal themselves in the light of day so they could be cleansed. Your mother or father was only answering this need and transmitting the message to your deep self.

So why not take advantage of the family meal to perform an intensive cleansing? This is the most practical solution. Instead of forcing the erroneous memories to emerge over several weeks or months, you can do a maximum cleansing in the space of a few hours. I am not suggesting you gather your family together for the sole reason of resolving present or past conflicts. Simply take advantage of a birthday, anniversary, or wedding to target the emotions that come up when you run into your uncle Robert or cousin Martin. Allow them to surge forth and acknowledge them.

You may say something like, "When I am with my aunt Josiane, she always tells me about her money problems. And it annoys me every time! I have the impression she thinks I am 'rolling in money.'"

Your interpretation of Aunt Josiane's remarks is surely mistaken, but the emotion you feel is quite real. It is at this very moment you need to set the Ho'oponopono process into action: "Forgive me. I am sorry for having inspired that reaction. Thank you, Aunt Josiane, for making this erroneous memory come to the surface. I love you, you the messenger, you who are part of me and of my family."

It is the same when you are in the presence of your sister who was just diagnosed with cancer and who continues to smoke one cigarette after another. It is no good to get angry or express your dismay when you have a formidable tool at your disposal: "I'm sorry, thank you, I love you." Repeat it as many times as necessary, and send love to your sister. When your judging attitude vanishes and your distress begins to fade, it becomes possible to communicate and work together so that this illness is no longer a burden on everyone.

Because the process of love has been put into motion, it will start casting its radiance on everyone around you. All those in your circle will feel this peace and their critical thoughts about you will shift course toward respect. The mirror that is your family can become the reflection of love, the one that will bond you.

Your soul has selected the best tools for your personal

development: your children, your parents, your grandparents, your brothers, your sisters, your uncles and aunts. So make the best use of them. They are there to help you grow.

Surprise!

I would like to give you a tip that helped me to put aside my expectation when I began practicing Ho'oponopono. At every cleansing, I would say, "I'm sorry, forgive me, thank you, I love you . . . surprise!"

"Surprise" was to indicate to my mind that something was definitely going to happen, but that I needed to just let it happen. I had no idea how it would arrive, nor where, nor when, nor what it would be, but I was convinced that a life surprise would follow the cleansing I had just made. The ego was content and kept busy by hearing the word *surprise,* which left my deep self the time necessary to concoct something unexpected for me. This never failed; an amazing variety of presents always arrived.

Today I no longer feel the necessity to say the word *surprise.* I've realized that I can have complete confidence and be without expectations. Astonishment is always present, only the certitude that the best solution will come to me has become more and more obvious.

Buddhism Always

Dr. Len speaks of the zero state as the objective of Ho'oponopono practice. I found an equivalent to this state in Buddhism with the notion of emptiness. One of the objectives of Buddhist teaching is to obtain this state of emptiness, for it is that state that will allow the reception of inspiration. It is necessary to grasp the value of being in this state of emptiness and how Ho'oponopono can offer valuable assistance.

Create Emptiness—Yes, But Why?

I am going to start by talking to you about the little voice that chants in your head in nagging, and not always positive, refrains. This is the mind. It starts talking at every possible opportunity, which is to say all the time. Moreover, this mind is quite incredible! It has an answer for everything and knows everything about everything. Even if it is wrong or has never been verified, it will still say it. I think of it like a child who wants to shock his friends by telling them stories he heard listening to adults, and whose real meaning he does not know. He speaks all the time, even if it is off topic.

This is how a constant flood of beliefs takes form and spreads through your mind. Over the course of the years since childhood, when your mind initially absorbed the words of those who raised you, this mind lurked in wait for everything that would reinforce what you had been told. It recorded all this new data on the hard drive of your beliefs, which it then repeated to you in endless loops.

The mind sorts through the information you take in and takes what it wants. When the rest is discarded, it will be recovered by your unconscious. Your deep self is connected to the unconscious mind, and thanks to that, it can wave flags to attract your attention in the case of a "system error"; in other words, in the event some erroneous beliefs have been acquired. It generally makes use of intuition and dreams, two tools that the mind detoured from their destination. Thus, when erroneous beliefs are received by your deep self, there is an immediate reaction that is not necessarily perceptible, as your mind is permanently chattering.

Nightmares can be extremely revealing signs. They indicate a "bug" in your system of beliefs that you have entirely missed seeing.

Your unconscious or deep self then rushes about like a madman trying to make you realize that a virus is present. It rings all the alarm bells, even going so far as to provoke serious incidents so you will reformat/cleanse your beliefs.

More concretely, the mind is the thing that keeps harping at you that you need to suffer to be beautiful, you have to work hard to make money, the rich are all thieves, illness only exists to make you suffer . . . all these common phrases that urge you to believe you are undeserving of happiness, that life is not worth the trouble, and you certainly are not either. In fact, it is a kind of ominous bird that you have engendered, and for your own reckoning.

 It is possible that behind the beating of your mind's black wings your deepest aspirations are hiding; those that reveal your inner beauty are a true value.

I think you are beginning to understand where I am trying to take you. Wouldn't it be in your best interest to silence the capricious child that is your mind to make the positive elements within you more prominent?

The vacuity, or emptiness, about which Dr. Len speaks is what makes it possible to tune in and follow the true path: this God that is within you, the one that allows you to realize yourself and shows you that this infelicitous event will permit you to follow your dream. This path will also lead you to look at your face and body as a wondrous realization, in which a complex assemblage of simple cells has created this incredible result—and thereby see in every living being the same marvelous crafting of life. Thanks to this inner emptiness you have created, you can finally receive the understanding that the universe is abundant, and that there is enough in profusion for everyone. You know that you deserve happiness.

So every time a negative phrase pops out of your mind's hat, wave your Ho'oponopono wand and transform it into a white dove, spreading its wings of love and gratitude. The emptiness it leaves behind will give way to peace, the pure emotion that engenders the joy of living.

Once the mind has been put at rest or into a meaningful state of peace, you have given yourself the possibility of being entirely receptive to the possibilities that enter your life. When your mind is constantly telling you, "There's so much misery on this earth," you see only the misery and forget to listen to the homeless who cross your path and especially need attention. When the mind starts drumming into your head, "I will never amount to anything," you prove it is right by never springing into action when opportunity knocks or by preferring to wait instead of inspiring more positive events. This is why there is nothing like creating emptiness to provide space for all possibilities. Creating a void allows divine action to arrive through your intermediary. You act with a guide who is more attentive to your needs. And how can you create this void if not by cleaning away the beliefs that have collected there again and again?

How to Create the Void

Here is a short story told by Wayne Dyer, author of best-selling books on the practical psychology of self-improvement, such as *Change Your Thoughts—Change Your Life*. It can allow you to memorize once and for all the value of using cleansing, in other words, Ho'oponopono, to create this emptiness.

The master told his disciple: "You must create the emptiness." The disciple responded that he did not know how.

His master then asked: "What do you do after you eat?"

"I digest," his disciple answered.

"No," his master retorted, "you do the dishes!"

This story was a revelation to me, full of common sense and humor.

Here and Now

Another element that makes this technique similar to Buddhist teachings is that every moment offers an excuse for practicing Ho'oponopono and consequently being present in the here and now. When you have suffered a trauma and take pains to do the cleansing immediately, you are in the present. When you have been upset by some news that has disturbed your mind and you do a cleansing, you are in the present.

 The future is conjecture, and the past has passed. Only the present counts.

For example, rather than imagining the worst while listening to your neighbor talk about the fuel shortage at your town's gas station, cleanse the memories that are activated in this moment. In this way you will avoid thinking about possibly having to cancel your trip planned for tomorrow, which would prevent you from seeing your children. There you are indulging in conjecture; in other words, you are in the future. But you could also be reminded of the last fuel-related strike, which prevented the restocking of your favorite stores, and that would mean dwelling in the past. In order to keep yourself in the present, the here and now, clean away those fears that are drowning you by simply saying, "Forgive me, thank you, I love you," and let calm settle through you. You will then be able to hear the rest of the conversation and learn that it involves a technical problem and the breakdown will last only two hours, the time necessary to restore the pumps to service.

As I described in this little story, the value of living in the present is to be in contact with reality, far from negative thoughts. Because these latter will appear when you are in the past (experiences that have already taken place) or the future (one of the mind's uncontrolled flights of fancy). Contrary to preconceived notions, you are not being a realist when referring to obsolete or imaginary data. You are in reality when you tune in to the here and now, to all the information coming in at that time, which will give you the whole story.

The same is true when you identify yourself with a past profession, as in, "I am a retired corporate executive." It is as if you were living with one foot in the past. You are only half alive.

"Children once respected their elders; those were the good old days." You are living in nostalgia, an idealized past. It makes it much more difficult to see the good aspects of your current life when your heart remains stuck in the past.

"Management is no longer as easygoing as before." You are

holding on to the advantages you lost when your company was sold. You are still in the past and cannot see the opportunities opening before you; you keep your eyes fixed on the resignations that followed. All of this is engendered because you are not in the present, connected with your deep self, which forms part of reality.

By anchoring yourself in the present, you become realistic. Far from anxieties and fears, you enter into the reality of the moment. Past experiences take their historic place in your memory files. They played their roles at a given time and have allowed you to construct your self.

 The past is not your life; it is one stone among others that helped you move forward. The future is first and foremost in your imagination before taking form.

This thought that you are creating from whole cloth can become a reality. Such power of the mind has been corroborated by many philosophers and scientists, so it is important to pay attention. The better the quality of thought, the better will be your future. And if you doubt your ability to create a bright future for yourself, let your unconscious mind of deep self do it for you. To help you keep a distance from fears, worries, and anxieties, do the cleansing that is activated by performing Hoʻoponopono. I would suggest in this case that it be done without moderation.

Love's Compassion

With Hoʻoponopono, you are led to look at each detail of your life more intensely and with greater love and compassion. Here is another path that mirrors religion.

"Thank you, I love you" is a very simple mantra to chant. These words also make it possible to establish contact with the Divine, with its Godhead. There is great value in pronouncing these words and repeating prayers over and over. You can achieve a state of automation in the brain by keeping your mind busy and, through this repetition, imprinting a new idea in it. Remain vigilant all the same, because words can have a double meaning. Your brain can interpret a phrase in several different ways—a *gilt band* can lead to *guilt banned*. This is just one example of how easy it is for your unconscious to reinterpret phrases, and prayers are no exception to this rule.

When my mind starts racing in reaction to an event, I have this cleansing tool that is on autopilot and works in perfect attunement with my convictions. It is the first technique I've found so easy to use. I think it is because these words, "Forgive me, thank you, I love you," offer few possibilities for interpretative errors.

By beginning with "Forgive me," you are opening the conversation with your deep self with the gift of self—your true value.

"Thank you" puts you in a trusting state; it puts you in an appreciative position for life and faith in life. This word is stronger than gratitude. It is gratitude to the present time, the past, or the time yet to come. Thanks to everything that lives—people, animals, nature, earth, and your creations. Yes, you have a great creative talent.

"I love you" is a phrase in which the word *love* rubs shoulders with *you*. There is the *I*, which, like an *eye*, can skim the surface or look deeply into things, such as your deep self. There is the *you* that represents the other, which is also my mirror, my own reflection, my unique nature. Love is the finest command my self can give.

"Thank you, I love you" is an invisible prayer said within to the person you overlook most often in your daily life—yourself. If these words don't anchor you to the best life has to offer, they come quite close.

To Be Christian

These fundamental principles of love can obviously be seen in the Christian religion, starting with the phrase, "Love your neighbor as yourself." What this intends to remind you is that the other person is the mirror of your life, and you are united by this sacred bond of love.

To Love Yourself
It is difficult to give others something you do not have. When you are filled with love, you can share this love with the humanity within you, that whole complex group that is as capable of causing you to suffer as it is of making you happy. The absence of judgment can be a path to attaining this feeling of peace, and with Ho'oponopono, you have a tool to help you get rid of judgments of all kinds.

When you judge your own actions by treating yourself like a loser or an idiot, for example, when you chastise yourself for spilling coffee on your shirt just before going to work, you lower your vibrational level and make yourself more and more susceptible to outside attacks. The depreciation of your own actions on a daily basis causes a reduction in both your immune system and your energy levels.

 Consider minor accidents in your life to be personal messages reminding you that you are not paying attention to yourself.

Instead of reading, listening to, or watching upsetting world news during your breakfast, take this time to concentrate on positive things and start your day off on the right foot. Focus on what is taking place outside your kitchen window. Study the shape of the morning clouds, watch life taking place on your street. Give yourself time to appreciate the moment.

By transforming minor everyday accidents into gratitude, you are sending yourself love. And as you fill yourself with love, you make yourself its transmitter to everyone whose path crosses yours.

So when your toast falls on the floor buttered-side down, a button pops off your shirt, your cup gets knocked over, or you find you have run out of cereal, send yourself love—"Forgive me, thank you, I love you."

To Forgive

The other element that often comes back with Ho'oponopono is the notion of forgiving every action made against you. It is a little like turning the other cheek after being slapped, in that you are using the "smacks" life sends you as pretexts for cleaning away your erroneous memories. This does not exempt the messenger from providing an explanation. Forgiveness is the acknowledgment that we all carry this violence within, and that it is necessary to break away from it in order to move forward in our evolution. Forgiveness is when you give someone else as well as yourself the opportunity to get back on the way of love.

 Forgiveness is not the same as submission.

When a young woman has her necklace snatched from her neck while walking home, she suffers a shock. Doing

Ho'oponopono in this case might seem inappropriate, but think of the fear that would be flooding her system and throwing her off balance. There might also be a feeling of guilt. These are the emotions the victim must detach herself from before she is able to take the most appropriate action in this situation.

When you remain mired in fear, you no longer dare leave home. When you take on the guilt, you no longer dare to file a complaint. The simple act of saying "Forgive me, thank you, I love you" gives you the possibility of restoring calm and recovering your spirits. You can tell yourself this: "Forgive me for inspiring temptation by sporting this piece of jewelry, forgive me for letting myself be victimized, forgive me for taking a less-safe street. Thank you for sending this memory of fragility, impotence, and anger. I love you, you who are the part of me that created this situation."

Forgive yourself for having been obliged to create this situation in order to uncover these memories so they could be cleansed. Forgive the universe for having been an accomplice to this, and forgive the thief for having been its hurtful messenger. And most importantly, send love to yourself and the universe.

You can next go to the police station to report the robbery without leaving out a single detail about the thief. Some of you might be saying to yourselves that there is no longer any need to lodge a complaint when the cleansing has been carried out properly, and on one hand that is true. But if the thief is arrested, he can perform Ho'oponopono in his turn.

When you feel you are going through a situation so violent that you are imagining ways to settle the problem while still in the grip of your anger, by forgetting the notion of forgiveness, you may encounter obstacles that will be more and more difficult to overcome.

A Little Illustration

It is 9 o'clock in the morning and you are late for a meeting, so you decide to take a shortcut. You suddenly have to slam on the brakes to avoid running a red light you failed to see in time. Your car is then hit from behind by another driver. You jump out, furious, to check the damage. On seeing your angry reaction to the crumpled bumper, the other driver starts shouting back at you. Spirits are so heated that neither of you sees the traffic jam forming behind you. Other drivers are honking and it is impossible to write a damage report because the driver who rear-ended you refuses to jeopardize his insurance rating for such a small mishap. Things escalate and the police are called in to take over, forcing you to get out your papers, not all of which are in order. The person you were planning to meet has been waiting for more than an hour by the time you telephone, at your wits' end.

Perhaps if you had introduced a note of compassion into this mishap, you would have realized that it was your inattentive driving that caused the other driver to hit his brakes late and scared him just as much as you. You could then have discussed matters calmly on the side of the road and amiably planned to get repairs from his mechanic to avoid any problems with his insurance agency. Then, in a perfect state of calm, you would have alerted your rendezvous that you would be arriving in just a few minutes, and you would make a note to yourself to get your papers updated.

The mirror of your life can take all forms, which is why it is worth respecting those who confront you. Forgiveness is a powerful tool to get yourself back on the path of love, especially when you use the magic words: "Forgive me for provoking this situation, thank you for having awakened this memory so that I could cleanse it, I love you, you the messenger."

 If you are a Christian, when you ask to be forgiven as you forgive those who trespass against you, Ho'oponopono will greatly help in activating this reflex action. For Christians and non-Christians alike, forgiveness is the key that opens the doors of love.

A Little Islam

Islamic rules ban the depiction of God's image, as well as images of any sentient being. Perhaps this can explain the presence of the magnificent frescoes and arabesques that adorn Muslim religious monuments. The artist's imagination is so rich and fertile that simply looking at his creation draws one into contemplative meditation. It may be a reason why mosques can be so inspiring. There are no idols to set the mind drifting; only an opportunity for introspection and better connection with the Divine. In the houses of those who live this faith, where no image can flatter the ego, it may be easier to admire the true mirror of God, who gives meaning to life.

All Are Spiritual

I see also in this absence a great presence, something truly crucial to our understanding. It is that God is boundless. No shape, no dimension, no place can represent Him. Nothing material can be identified with Him.

I am going to go even further by adding that just as God cannot be accurately depicted, the same is true for humans and all creatures of the earth. Couldn't a far nobler definition of the human being be found in this metaphor? I'm referring to the immaterial divinity in each of us. We are not simply physical bodies, but much, much more—we are spiritual. The creatures and the Creator are united in the universal energy that enables us to circulate in this world.

 You are a divine being in the most magnificent sense of the word. You are much more than a profession, a father, or a mother; you are more than the illness that afflicts you; you are part of God.

In this way, Ho'oponopono opens the door to an incredible rediscovery of human nature. Not only does it oblige you to look within, it also asks you to give yourself all the gratitude and love you deserve as the spiritual entity you are.

Getting Your Bearings Back

When I visited Marrakesh and heard the Islamic call to prayer, I could not help but smile. Five times a day I was being reminded that I am truly a spiritual being. Five times a day I was reconnected to my sacred self. Five times a day I found peace.

Christian churches rarely ring the bells of spirituality. Modern society has transformed these appeals into communication tools that urge you to consume and make you forget your true vocation.

Under the pretext of secularism, the divine part of you has been camouflaged, and this loss of connection is behind your irrepressible desire to fill your living space with objects. You have replaced love with pleasure, a feeling that does not last and which you maintain by means of technological gadgets and fleeting romantic affairs. Newspaper, television, and social media ads have replaced the chiming of church bells; the village is now animated by a virtual rhythm. How can you get your spiritual bearings back in a world where everything can be ordered online?

There are several ways to establish communication with your sacred self. Religion is just one path; there are a good many others. To remind yourself of your true nature, you can use everything that refers you back to the best part of yourself. It is fruitless to try to compare yourself to the ideals created by the media; you are both unique and share an intense connection with all other creatures in the universe. Remind yourself that this connection is a divine bond of love. Others have just as much love in them and are just as spiritual as you, even your neighbor who bellows out his window at two o'clock in the morning. It is just that by placing itself in a material form, this vibration of love offers all the particles of life a chance to live. Then they begin colliding into one another in this huge earthly chaos. However, they possess the power to transmit as one in a song of peace. In order to reach this point, they need to find their spiritual road again. You can use reminders to love, such as "Forgive me, thank you, I love you," to bring you back to this path.

Creative Creatures

"The twenty-first century will be spiritual or it will not be." This sentence has taken on its full meaning at the time I am writing these lines, because at this time bookstore shelves are covered with the spiritual experiences of men and women in quest of their divinity. We who look at the world differently are growing in number. We realize that fighting an institution is not enough and that the thirst for power will never be quenched in the material world; we need to go further.

The true exploration that each human being on this planet was meant to make was to visit the depths of his or her soul, the inner self with its infinite capabilities.

You have also realized that everything that exists comes from thoughts produced by others before you, which are taking form today. Every invention was first hatched in the mind of an individual before it appeared in your hands.

Your ideas are just as strong. They first live in your mind before appearing to everyone. Herein lies your creative power. You have created this world. You have given life to all these contradictions. This is why you should stop judging what surrounds you. You have created the best situation to propel your evolution. The proof is that when you have a problem, it concerns you, no one else.

This notion can seem difficult to accept. However, I can promise you that it is quite real and also very comforting. Once you realize that you are the principal actor in your own life in the broadest sense of the term, that your actions have real repercussions in this world, then you are no longer a victim. You can abandon the role of feeling powerless and subject to events. You are entering a dimension in which all, absolutely everything, is possible.

The extent of what is possible is as vast as the universe, and the universe is quite large.

What Is Outside Comes from the Inside

I will resume my journey on the continent of Asian cultures with *feng shui,* a system of harmonizing your energy with your environment. The geomancers who practice this ancestral Chinese art use *qi* (life force) energy to improve lives spiritually and materially. Qi circulates throughout the entire universe and connects all individuals. This should certainly remind you of something.

This universal energy that enters bodies and thoughts is permeated in its travels by the varied forms that nature has placed on its route. Its quality and role change in accordance with places and orientation. It requires an educated calculation to determine the type of qi that is entering your home and the use of the five elements—water, metal, fire, earth, and wood—to balance it and make it harmonious.

The precept "What is outside comes from the inside" is a Western interpretation of this art. For purists of traditional feng shui, it is the environment that influences people and not the opposite. Qi energy circulates in the environment and natural elements (mountains, rivers) providing the energetic "relief" of the site. To draw the best influences from it, the individual arranges the five elements in such a way as to strengthen or reduce the power of yin (female energy) and yang (masculine energy). In this way, qi permits the inhabitants to preserve their own energy. The five elements are used to optimize and compensate for the weak points of their dwelling.

My experience as a feng shui consultant has allowed me to make the following observation: you and I influence the environment. A real interaction occurs between a place and its inhabitants. My observations have enabled me to grasp the extent to which each of us is 100 percent the creator. This is a powerful point in common with the concept of Ho'oponopono. And in feng shui as in life, what has been made can be unmade.

Inner Creators

Environmental creativity comes into play once you have personalized a place.

Decoration is a way of creating, of inventing an ambiance, and in this endeavor you will place everything you adore in what I call decor-ador-ation. This concerns your home and workplace equally. Decorative ornaments, furniture, the color of the walls and drapes, the function of each room, and the way you organize them are all creations.

The same holds true in a yard or garden. The flowers and trees you plant, fruits and vegetables you grow, and the places you choose for planting are all ways of creating the painting that surrounds you.

You are an artist painting your life. The house is the canvas and the objects are the tubes of paint you blend together and apply, just as you would use a paintbrush.

And because you arrange your space by using your culture, traditions, desires, and dreams, you display to the world what you hold inside of you. This is how everything that surrounds you comes from your "interior."

I would add that choosing one residence over another, renting a store or office to start a business, or even investing in a vacation home are all choices that also form part of creativity's subtle equation. Some will say it was a case of love at first sight, or make a rational case for a good quality/price ratio, but the elements are always very subjective and you alone decide their value. Once again, you are the actor and creator of this decision.

When you envision moving into a space, you make your selection based on your own criteria of the moment. Whether you live on Charity Place or Liberty Street is also very revealing. Your postal address, far from being insignificant, can reveal some unconscious desire you wish to transmit. Here again, you have created clues for understanding the transformation you will find there.

You are so inclined to think you have no power over what surrounds you that you forget just how much of a real impact you have. I am speaking about your house, of course, but it is also true of the town you have chosen to live in, your region, your country, and even your planet. You have no idea of the great power you wield.

I would also like to stress that you are an excellent creator of generating perfect creations. The house, region, or country in which you have chosen to live suits you perfectly. Yet it can be hard to believe in the perfection of your choices when catastrophes seem to follow on each other's heels as soon as you move into the space. How is it possible to accept this theory when your closest neighbors are noisy students whose nocturnal habits and music leak freely through the walls of your apartment? What can be said about the terrible odors from the reprocessing plant that invade your office just a few days after you finalize your purchase of it? All of this contributes to great skepticism about your creative abilities, and a feeling of guilt can then intrude.

The most arduous part consists of accepting these phenomena as developmental tools and not as unfair, insurmountable obstacles. Ho'oponopono is there to put these events back in their proper place, removing you from your tendency to behave like a victim and helping you to take back your role as actor-creator.

These signs that upset your daily life are electrical discharges to make you react, in order to bring you back to the very essence of your life.

Household accidents may be signs that you need to let go of your material interests and concentrate on your inner realization. Could noisy neighbors be a ploy to rouse you from the torpor that habit has installed in your life, which you maintain at the expense of your happiness? And unpleasant odors may be openly telling you that something does not "smell" right in your life, or more simply that you do not "sense" this new customer that just came in. Everything has a meaning.

Doing Ho'oponopono not only entails acceptance of events, it also means acceptance of your magnificent creative power, the one that helped you craft an environment favorable to your development. In this way it is easier to thank yourself for having stepped in to open new perspectives. The cleansing of feelings of guilt and anger gives you the opportunity to look at your life in a new way and leave room for the best solutions. This could be moving to a new space, perhaps in a different city. In all respects, you will continue your evolution there.

Attraction and Ho'oponopono

From feng shui to the power of attraction is but one mystical step. This way of operating is a kind of inescapable universal law. To sum up the law of attraction, we can simply note that violence attracts violence and gestures of love attract compassion. This is an experience each of us has lived through simply by reaping what we sow.

When you have grasped that the environment is an emanation of your persona and the qi energy circulating in everything, and that the universe can as easily assume negative or positive aspects based on what it encounters, it is easy to imagine the impact that one can have on the other.

The quality of the energy that rules your house depends on its orientation and exterior environment, whether it is natural or artificial (mountains, rivers, apartment buildings, roads). When a house receives harmful energies, it is necessary to counter this flow by playing with the way the interior is organized. Making your home a snug and cozy protective nest for your entire family is one remedy. In this way you can transform the negative energy into a beneficial ray for all those living in the house. Another aspect, no less important, is that once this energy has been transformed positively it causes changes at the vibrational level. When this happens, the harmful energies that surround your house are summoned to other locales, leaving the field clear for beneficial rays.

More concretely, when the inhabitants of a place decide to adjust their living arrangements using feng shui in order to optimize the site for the manifestation of their dreams, their goals are rapidly achieved.

Sometimes I also see a change take place in the thinking process of the inhabitants. The principal cause of this change is the improved energy circulation in the house. This may correspond to the circulation of the inhabitants who now have no obstacles to hinder them; for example, someone now has free access to a work table. The house glides smoothly and there is no disorder allowing energy to stagnate and diminish in quality. Useless items have been disposed of at yard sales and recycling centers, and the closets and cellar store only what is necessary, with room for future material acquisitions. The decor is positive and energy enhancing for everyone living in the space. This is how they will increase their optimism and establish their confidence, and opportunities will start knocking. They will attract luck, and the success of their every endeavor will be assured. The phenomenon of attraction has been set in place.

Sometimes, too, changes are so subtle that people do not see them and they become impatient and begin to doubt the soundness of their plan. Dark ideas begin to form and attention is diverted toward concerns that are felt to be more in tune with one's mood of the moment. Some people dive into social media to pass time, others launch into a complete makeover of the garage to feel useful, while still others decide to clean the house from top to bottom every day to avoid feeling guilty. They may procrastinate about completing the documents required to continue a project, until the day it becomes urgent.

Doubt then gives way to self-depreciation and your plans become buried under the pile of laundry to be ironed and books to be put in order. You may tell yourself, "It is not worth talking anymore about this, it was an idiotic idea and I am a complete loser to have ever believed it would work." The law of attraction is still working, but because the notions of "good" and "evil" utterly escape it, it attracts back to your house what you sent, and in this case it was not your best, as I am sure you realize.

It is the same thing for energies, or qi. Stagnant places capture stagnant energies; walls that have witnessed tragedies attract perverse energies. Breaking the vicious circle that has been established becomes necessary, and it is changing the energetic level of the space that makes the arrival of beneficial qi possible. The same is true when you break away from negative emotional habits. Once you take off the demeaning role of victim, you enter into a dynamic in which everything becomes possible. Make room for abundance and prosperity in your home and in your life.

As explained in the principle of the law of attraction, the emotional aspect is quite important. The negative feelings you are drowning in attract more negative emotions, which trigger increasingly unpleasant situations. However much you resist allowing your emotions to guide you, you regularly fall into the trap. Fortunately, Ho'oponopono is there to pull you out of a fix by giving you back the reins of your life.

 When emotions have gained control over your everyday life and you are entangled in their net, a good cleansing of both your house and mind is essential.

When you think the world is unfair, that your spouse or partner is wrong, and that your boss is completely irrational, it is no longer you who is managing your life but your fears, worries, and doubts. The erroneous beliefs they cause to surge back to the surface can be erased, and with Ho'oponopono, every difficult situation serves as a pretext for cleansing: "Forgive me, I am sorry I created this doubt, I did not know I had this inside . . . thank you, thank you for bringing it out into the open so I could clean it . . . I love you, the one who made me doubt . . . I love myself for having identified this belief so I could clean it away once and for all."

The phrase "Thank you, I love you" is fully sufficient to dissolve it completely, and in case there is any doubt about the cleansing, repeat it until this negative emotion makes way for good sense, the one with a loving gaze that sees beyond all fear.

All of these emotions that generate more difficulties than

solutions can be swept away with a single phrase. You will rediscover the best energies, thereby attracting the best solutions. It is an indispensable tool for making the universal law of attraction effective and positive. I cannot help but recommend its use, for it will make the enormous potential in this world accessible to everyone. It is an essential complement to the realization of your plans and dreams, a key to open a universe of all possibilities to you. And, as I suggested earlier, the universe is truly vast, so just imagine the possibilities.

Attraction: Operating Instructions

To use the law of attraction in the optimal way, you need to realize that this law makes no distinction between "good" and "bad." It is constantly active, no matter the person, place, or type of thought. The best means of attracting positive events, thanks to this quantum phenomenon, is to continuously emit positive thoughts. This is something that is not, a priori, imaginable to the majority of people living on the planet.

The tool of Ho'oponopono is most useful in this rediscovery of our creative potential. It makes it possible to clean away negative thoughts that are nothing other than erroneous memories. It works like a shower of love where you have only to say "Forgive me, thank you, I love you" to work the faucet. Once they have been cleansed, these memories are dissolved forever. The space is free for positive openness.

The phenomenon of attraction is implemented quickly thanks to the connections that are made on positive ideas. The greater the cleansing, the clearer the visualization will be. You can visualize images of success and fulfillment more easily with Hoʻoponopono. Whenever a doubt emerges, cleanse. Whenever a fear strikes you, cleanse. Whenever you are feeling impatient, cleanse. Whenever a negative emotion occurs, cleanse.

And just as you trust in this phenomenon of attraction, you will have no expectations about the way in which it will appear.

Some will say that you must have faith, others that you must trust life. I am telling you that the practice of Hoʻoponopono is first and foremost not having any expectations about results. Because the last thing you need to be worrying about, when you are drowning in problems, is details about the result.

You know what you need. You need to live in abundance, not resolve your money problems. You need to be healed, not find the miracle cure for this disease. You need to share your life with your kindred soul, not live with a creature of style. You need work that matches your skills, not this "job" that you saw in the classifieds.

Send out a positive request and visualize the film of your dream realized successfully, while cleaning away your fears. As the days flow past, let life handle it. Everything will come at the right time, in the best possible way for you.

Hoʻoponopono Resonates in Each of Us

To finish my explanation about the law of attraction, I will bring you deeper into the subtle world, a place where answers can be found to many of your questions.

Because you and I are made of flesh and blood, it is easy to deny the thoughtful, reflective parts of ourselves. My ideas are not contained in an organ; they rather seem to come from somewhere up high, outside of my head. I do not need an MRI to grasp the fact that my brain is a receiver. It stores data, which is then distributed throughout my body in an electrochemical form.

Bolstered by this observation, I also envisioned the possibility that, as in feng shui, information can be more or less good in quality, depending on the state of those who are sending it. I emphasize emotional "state" and not the individual person. We are all similar when it comes to constitution, health problems, and the experiences that create differences on a physical level, which do not make us better or worse than anyone else.

Emotions can inspire joy or force the reemergence of erroneous beliefs that will make you feel anxious. This is where your thoughts can pose a problem to others. You are equipped with radar that allows you to detect "ideas that are in the air" and put yourself in tune with the person in front of you. Physical posture is another means of communication, but we perceive the energy emanating from an individual in a more subtle fashion. The release of pheromones seems to provide a scientifically satisfactory answer to this phenomenon. However, this hormonal release is triggered because the body commanded it to happen, so I am asking who gave the order. The further back we trace a process, the more plain it is that it was clearly a thought that triggered this whole mechanism.

We have all had the experience of sometimes feeling something unsettling when we are speaking to someone we do not know. Our sixth sense is advising us to be extra cautious around a certain individual, or conversely, a friendship can blossom in an instant.

The energy you transmit with your thoughts is clearly felt

by everyone, like an amplified phenomenon, when you are in the grip of an intense emotion such as anger, which will ensure that you encounter only aggressive people.

One example is driving behavior, because in the car we are extremely exposed to all kinds of emotions. Have you ever noticed how when you are annoyed by the driver in front of you, there are more people behind you honking their horns? Likewise, the more frightened you are to pass on a two-lane road, the more cars you see coming from the other direction. The more you curse the driver in front of you who keeps slamming on his brakes, the more likely you are to receive insults from the motorcyclist trying to pass you.

Conversely, when you are merrily singing along with your favorite tune, the easier the road appears to be. All the other drivers seem incredibly polite and all the lights turn green just as you reach them. Just luck? Perhaps. Being in tune with your sacred self is more like luck than you could possibly imagine.

> Your emotional state is your vibrational state. Your vibrations give birth to those famous mirrors—other people. Their reaction is nothing other than your inner state.

Let me say it again: There is nothing like a good cleansing of negative emotions to put you in tune with real life. You will meet more and more considerate, caring people who resonate with your frequency by placing yourself in Ho‘oponopono mode. This is how the law of attraction works. You attract what you give out, then vibrate with all that is the best within you.

How to Change the World

After you have read this book, you should have some ideas on how to change the world. I have provided you with a trail—it starts within you and ends by changing you. Here is the answer to this riddle: Change the world by changing yourself!

Just by changing the way you look at the world you are changing it, only that is not enough. The vision you have of life, society, people, the stock exchange, and style is your own, unique vision. It depends on your education and your personality. Spiritual practices allow you to attain compassion and tolerance, which is a formidable means of changing the way you look at others, but there is also something that serves as a tiny irritant. This tiny piece of grit might be judgment.

 You can change the world by changing yourself.

And yes, I judge you, you judge me, you are judging yourself all the time. And not necessarily consciously, but with fleeting thoughts that appear and disappear as quickly as they are born.

A Choice Selection of Judgmental Thoughts

"I prefer her in her black dress, it suits her better."

"That haircut! The hairdresser did a terrible job."

"Why can't that guy get ahead?"

"Green beans again? We had them last night."

"I can't stand the sight of this guy. Why is he still on television?"

Little barbs that emerge from your mind are about as gentle as the stroke of an abrasive sandpaper on a new leather sofa. It leaves traces on the sofa that will serve as a reminder of this painful moment to whomever sits on it. This sofa is your relationship with others; the marks are the traces of your judgment of them. It is impossible to retreat, excuses are not enough; it is like a blockage. You realize that it irritated the person, and you are sincerely sorry, but it just came out on its own.

How is it possible to get out of this vicious cycle in which your most acerbic and indelicate thoughts settle in for the long haul? You could ask those around you to think like you do, but even with the strongest will in the world, it would take them years and years of work to understand all the subtle connections that take place inside you when you're confronted by the billions of events life can throw at you. Even the most powerful computer cannot compile a list of every possible reaction you might experience during your lifetime. But let's agree that if a computer could pull off this feat, this realization would still need to be incorporated by the seven billion individuals whose paths you might possibly cross in your lifetime. Taking it a step further, we would need to record the seven billion hypothetical permutations for each individual on the planet. I am convinced that you and I carry inside all the information that is circulating through the universe, but at the current stage in humanity's evolution, we are still a long way from being able to make full use of this power. Thus, for the moment, it is impossible to achieve this kind of training.

So I suggest a simpler method, which will require a little of your time but will ensure that your life grows lighter as your mind grows more open. This technique consists of changing our nature if we want the attitude of the world to change toward us, to borrow Gandhi's sentiments.

 If you want love, be loving. If you want peace, be peaceful. If you wish to see joy, be joyful. This might seem completely basic as principle and fact, and it is. But it is also highly effective.

To revisit the topic of judgment, there is of course a way to get some perspective on this extremely cumbersome phenomenon that prevents you from living in love, peace, and joy. It is acceptance.

Accepting the unacceptable is the key to letting go of judgment once and for all. Here, too, it is something other than submission to events. Because submission is inaction, and because life is movement, it is in your best interest to take actions that will ensure you are in accord with it. Acceptance consists of approaching life peacefully rather than with anger or grief. It is a way of preserving your energy instead of watching it be frittered away in the torment caused by hatred or depression. Thanks to acceptance, you can keep a cool head and obtain miraculous results from others.

Judgment is the pebble I carried in my shoe for a long time. It comes back, the bugger, when I start wandering through the no-man's land of my mind.

I learned some time ago that the absence of judgment can guarantee peace, while the opposite can set the stage for a long sleepless night.

During a family discussion about the necessity of having an army to defend one's family, friends, and neighbors, and one's country from enemy nations, I saw the extent to which the mind could outstrip reason. The person I was speaking with stated that the taking of hostages justified the use of deadly force by an army against aggressors. In his opinion, this was a necessary action to protect our nation's tranquility. "Our army should defend us; the soldiers are risking their lives for us." He would have enjoyed being one of these heroes. But these hostage-takers have also been attacked in their country, and they took the actions they did to protect *their* family and nation. I was not able to find the right words to tone down this discussion, as taking a life is unacceptable to me.

Our differing values obstructed this discussion. What is good and what is evil? Who is right and who is wrong? I never have answers for these kinds of questions. I know in my depths that every life has its own reason for being, and that it is precious and unique. It deserves respect, no matter what form it takes. I had forgotten to enter love that night. The conflict that sprang up disrupted my night, and by early morning I realized that it was through accepting the opinions of others, violent as they might be, that I could accept the part of myself that had created this encounter, this mirror. Somewhere deep inside I had a fear of other people that could lead me to kill. I can assure you that it is as difficult to write this as it is to accept.

In this case, acceptance and the absence of judgment are the only belief systems to involve. Otherwise the ego gets the upper hand and ensures you have a permanent falling out with the person who brought the message. Denigrating the other person and trying to protect yourself prevents you from seeing and accepting the shadow within yourself. This small sensation of safety provided by your rejection of the other person is illusory, because a sense of discomfort will always come up when the other person is mentioned. An erroneous belief has just been born: "I have better judgment than he does."

To facilitate the transition to acceptance, the phrase "Forgive me, thank you, I love you" never served me so well as it did on that night. To have trust in life requires that you also place your trust in other people's choices, accepting that they are no better or worse than your own. They belong to them, and this is how I am able to love these individuals.

The second effect is self-acceptance of your own responsibility for events, even the least glorious. Ridding yourself of a judgmental attitude allows you to reach this place.

In fact, the best moment was when I sent myself love, an unconditional love that radiated out to the person who had permitted me to attain this blessing.

Saying Thank You

When a neighbor offers you flowers from her garden, when your eighteen-year-old son gently hugs you, when a sales clerk makes you a gift of a few pennies on your purchase, when your car starts right up in freezing weather, when your boss tells you to take the afternoon off, and when the pain you were feeling fades away while you nap—these are all perhaps signs that you are entering into a new kind of movement. You are on the road to serenity. You start off with baby steps, than with long, flexible strides you enter the great marathon of life. As the miles flow by, you are going to discover your abilities, the ones you no longer believed would emerge, that reveal your amazing power to endure and surpass yourself. It is a sacred moment when you discover that limits no longer exist.

I admit that I am still astonished when I see this reserve of abilities that dwells in each of us. This abundance is everywhere, not just in the body you think you know so well. It continues to surprise us with its unexpected healing abilities, as if it were the mailbox holding a reimbursement check that will prevent a bank overdraft this month. You can go to great lengths when you are vibrating with all your love and gratitude toward the little unexpected things in life. The more thankful you are for what you have and how it fulfills you, the more abundance will nurture you. The more love you give to life, the more it will return. Sometimes I tell myself it is almost too much. It is so beautiful that it makes me shy, and I no longer know how to respond to these abundant gifts.

 Welcoming this bliss with an open heart has been another way for me to use Ho'oponopono. I have learned to say "thank you." Thank you to all the opportunities that are opening to me, to what my life is creating today, and to all it has built over the years. I feel this gratitude as an expression of my deep self, whose enormous potential I am uncovering.

I think back to all those years when I was listening to spiritual teachers of all faiths speak of the fulfillment to be found in the act of thanking God. At that time I hadn't grasped the necessity of that act. It was incomprehensible to me to say "thank you" to something I could not see, something I could barely feel, and something that made me go through so many ordeals.

The somewhat unique experience that I have had with the practice of Ho'oponopono has allowed me to be open to other methods of personal development, to accept my true nature and openly display my talents, discover wonderful personalities, and start projects and complete many.

When I realize all this, I have no other choice but to thank God, the universe, or intention with all my heart for having allowed me to fulfill so many dreams. And it is far from being over. I have the impression of being in the early stages of awareness, as I feel such power in this creative energy.

 Thank you!

Thank you, thanks to this creative energy for being present, thanks to all whose paths have crossed mine and allowed me to become aware of its existence. Thanks to all the mirrors who are other people and an emanation of my unconscious mind. Thanks to my ego for exhibiting these erroneous memories that I discard with love. Thank you, dear reader, for being alive and for permitting this book to live.

How to Live through Moments of Doubt

Among you are people who have been practicing Ho'oponopono for several weeks or for several months and, despite this, continue to be the target of strong electrical discharges from life. These clashes arrive without warning. Just when you are strolling self-confidently along the path of love, in a flash you suddenly find yourself on a mountain of doubt and guilt.

You have conscientiously cleared away the no-man's land that was once your mind so you could transform it into a garden. You have gotten rid of the weeds of negative emotion to make a place for a magnificent park in which trees of serenity are flourishing, flowerbeds of kindness are carefully maintained, and the lawn of tranquility is impeccable. So when someone drops a peel in your garden, you are unable to see anything but this odious litter staining your paradise. This vision becomes the focus of all your attention.

After this bucolic metaphor, here are a few leads to help you better understand this phenomenon that sends you feelings of guilt and other unpleasant emotions just at the time you are meticulously cleaning away your erroneous memories.

Perhaps it is because for several weeks you have been experiencing a lighter vibration than you had with old habits, and when you return to the tone of the past, the difference is so intense that you find it impossible to live any longer in this former vibration. It no longer corresponds to you. You have become increasingly removed from this thought system, so when it reappears, its intrusion is so disharmonious it can no longer be tolerated.

Perhaps when old battles show up in their dirty boots within the crystalline decor you have constructed it is difficult for you to recognize them. They make a stain on your life. It is impossible for your ego to camouflage them behind the curtains of resentment you have been cleaning since you began doing Ho'oponopono. They are quite visible, with no mask or embellishments, and they come to shake you up just when calm has begun to reign.

 Perhaps you have also forgotten how chaotic your life was before this great cleansing?

Imagine that you have spent your entire life in a city that was ceaselessly pounded by bombs and attacks, and that peace had been restored after a great cleansing. You have just found the key to greater harmony in your life thanks to Ho'oponopono, and you are finally living in the city of peace. The only thing is that a few renegades remain in the underground passageways. They were invisible during the poundings of the past, but they have just revealed their presence by tossing a grenade into your street.

Surprise and ensuing fear are justified. However, it is in your best interest to continue the cleansing so that love takes over the underground areas of your life. Otherwise emotional chaos could again overwhelm you.

This is how you can learn the practice of Ho'oponopono. The cleansing is first made on the surface and the sensation of calm it creates becomes more perceptible as you continue this work. The loud "boom" that comes just when you are smiling at life with all your heart is in fact as intense as the preceding erroneous memories you have discarded. In the peaceful landscape that has become your life, this boom seems like the explosion of an atom bomb. You had never noticed it until now because it had always gone off in the middle of stray shots that were pounding your city.

When I look at the people around me who are still living in this emotional chaos, I challenge myself to clean the image they are sending me until I have restored my inner peace while watching them live their lives. I enter into communion with this disorder that I, too, have experienced for many years. I reconcile with it through these individuals, and I send them all the love they deserve so that I can allow myself to love who I was and who they are today. Acceptance and the absence of judgment and expectations have become essential to my maintaining this peaceful state. This, too, is what Ho'oponopono is—the reconnection in love with everything that nourished you and allowed you to become who you are today.

Ho'oponopono Every Day

What I like about the practice of Ho'oponopono is that it can be integrated into all lifestyles. Whether you are a believer, an atheist, or simply a seeker, this tool is extremely useful to all who desire to evolve.

This is because human beings need to know where they are coming from, who they are, and why they are here. Each of us has a question inside that needs an answer. The search for meaning is a powerful motor that gives wings to life. Its intensity varies only based on the will of the individual. It is up to each person to decide where this engine should lead, knowing full well that this motor is propelled by boundless positive energy.

Why is it so powerful? It is quite simply because of the deep self that is there, throbbing with joy at the idea of helping you discover the magic of life. This motor is therefore plugged into the boundless reservoir of the universe, with an abundance of the fuel called love.

And what is this love? It is the grand flow that traverses the universe and which some people believe to be the power of God. Others call it the power of intention, or qi. What I can tell you is that it is everywhere, and it is what connects you to the universe. So just as each of us on this planet is connected to the universe, you and I are connected. This union is not metaphorical; it is really there, though impalpable and extremely present. You know that satellites beam across the entire surface of the earth and can connect you with other people, so think of yourself as a relay antenna. You hold an inexhaustible power that is sent to you by all the satellites of the universe, and you can transmit it.

How do you transmit love? It is fairly simple, in fact. It is by connecting you to the "computer chip" that serves as a connection with the universe. The chip is your deep self, your inner deity, and the access code is "I'm sorry, forgive me, thank you, I love you." Next you let the universe, God, or intention do what it does. That's all.

The thing that is so incredible about Ho‘oponopono is that this approach does not replace any other developmental process. It does much better than that, as it can accompany every technique that follows this direction.

For example, when you are using tools such as meditation, yoga, or qi gong to establish a sense of peace within you and you start feeling your mind drifting, Ho‘oponopono allows you to regain the inner concentration that peace gives you. "I'm sorry, forgive me, thank you, I love you." This will help you pull yourself together when your ego is putting up too many excuses for why you should not dive into meditation.

Another important point is that you do not need anybody else in order to do Ho‘oponopono. No guru, therapist, or priest can do it in your place. The predominant aspect of this method is the autonomy of thought. Each time a conflict arises in your presence, it is up to you to decide whether or not to cleanse it. No one else steps in or makes the decision in your place. You are the only actor.

In fact, it is an element that immediately called out to me in this practice. I was seduced by the idea of not having to ask anyone for anything to free myself from guilt, jealousy, fear, and greed. I just needed to be attuned to myself.

The other notion that gave me the desire to say "I'm sorry, forgive me, thank you, I love you" was that of my own responsibility in events, or rather my creative participation in their making. I no longer had any reason to have it in for anyone; I simply had to look at the facts for what they are: personal messages to help us evolve. This allowed for a breathtaking increase in energy. Imagine all the energy we expend in resentment, anger, and sorrow. No more useless fatigue, no more irritations that go on for days and months—what a huge gain in time!

Over the months and years of my Ho'oponopono practice, I've made new discoveries. This is because the cleansing of erroneous memories and the empty space they left was to inspiration's advantage. All this took place through synchronicities—those things that happen at an opportune moment because your unconscious mind has permitted them to exist in your surroundings. You know that there is no coincidence when you reach this level of understanding. Everything becomes a message.

From the book you just chose to the conversation with a stranger in the supermarket, by way of the e-mail that gives you an idea to write about in your next article, it is perpetually active movement. It is right there in front of you, showing you that abundance is in fact within arms' reach.

 Wouldn't this abundance be transported by the flow of the universe, or the power of God, or that divine energy whose true name you have guessed? Yes, it really is that—abundance travels on the wings of love.

Ho'oponopono and You

Nathalie Bodin Lamboy

Dear Reader, I am sure you have now realized that the practice of Hoʻoponopono is an art of living that needs to be tried in order to grasp its true content. I therefore invite you to begin this practice at the most opportune time for you.

The phrase "I'm sorry, forgive me, thank you, I love you" is a foundation that you can build on and embellish, depending on your mood. There are no rules. For some, "Thank you, I love you" will be enough; for others, like me, improvising can have a greater impact for this cleansing. The most important thing is to connect with your inner power. This is a creative power that dwells permanently within you; you simply have to call on it to form the connection.

This connection to love is a return to our true nature. There are three steps that can help you to achieve this feat. The first is to fulfill your personal mission, thanks to the elimination of erroneous memories, as explained by Jean Graciet. The second is acceptance of your dark side, in other words the duality that is a human characteristic, and which Luc Bodin explored in this book. And finally, the third is to be in gratitude toward this so-perfect universe, which, for me, Nathalie Bodin Lamboy, was a wonderful discovery through Hoʻoponopono.

Now that you are in possession of several keys to finding peace with yourself and pushing all your potential forward, I will leave you to discover your own answers to the questions that reading this book may inspire.

And as you have reached the last page, please do not look at this as a conclusion, rather consider this book as a preface to your life—a kind of introduction to the chapters to follow that you, yourself will write.

I simply hope that *The Book of Ho'oponopono* will give you a taste for adventure and offer you guidance in your exploration of life.

May you have beautiful discoveries.

 "Thank you, I love you."

Notes

Chapter 1. From the Origins of the Practice to Today

1. Tipping, *Radical Forgiveness,* 11.
2. Clerc, *The Gift of Forgiveness,* 35.

Chapter 2. From the Psychological World to Quantum Reality

1. Schützenberger, *Exercises pratiques;* Del Castillo, *La psychogénéalogie appliqué.*
2. Drouot, *Nous sommes tous immortels.*
3. Valois, "Le rôle des phénomènes épigénétiques."
4. Quotimed.com, "Exposition in utero à la pollution."
5. Dumas, "Epigénétique."
6. Anastasiou and Mandelbaum, "Risque épigénétique et assistance médicale à la procreation," 190–99.
7. Dumas, "Epigénétique."
8. Sciences et Avenir.com, "Variabilité génétique."
9. Institut Curie and CNRS, "Epigénétique et cancer."
10. Schwitzgedel, "Role de l'épigénétique dans le diabète et la croissance."

11. Valois, "Le rôle des phénomènes épigénétiques."

12. Ibid.

13. Ornish, Magbanua, Weidner, et al., "Changes in Prostate Gene Expression," 8369–74.

14. Dumas, "Epigénétique."

15. Popenon's remarks were recorded by Gregg Braden. See www .greggbraden.com/video/.

16. *Nexus,* 44–45.

17. Sauvageot, *Les yeux d'Uranie.*

18. Suggested reading on the Cathars includes Blum, *Les Cathares, du Graal au secret de la mort joyeuse*; Genel, *La voie parfait*; Griffe, *Les Cathares*; Pahin, *Le Baptême d'esprit.*

19. Astier, "Energie noire, la grande inconnue."

20. Chopra, *Quantum Healing.*

21. Emoto, *Hidden Messages in Water;* Emoto, *Miracle of Water.*

22. Experiment cited by Ransford in "Un monde déconcertant" as well as on the site www.passeportsante.net with the reference Cha, Wirth, and Loba, "Does Prayer Influence the Success of In Vitro Fertilization-Embryo Transfer?"

23. Harris et al., "A Randomized Controlled Trial of the Effects of Remote, Intercessory Prayer."

24. See Benson, www.relaxationresponse.org.

25. Fowler and Christakis, "Dynamic Spread of Happiness."

26. Holder of a doctorate in science, Jacqueline Bousquet is an honorary researcher of the CNRS (www.arsitra.org) and author of several books such as *Au Coeur du vivant* (St. Michel du Bologne, France: Saint-Michel, 1992) and *Le réveil de la conscience* (Paris: Guy Trédaniel, 2003).

27. Science & Vie, "La vie serait quantique: sens de l'odorat," 64–65.

28. See Luc Bodin's book, *Préparez-vous au changement,* which can be downloaded for free or purchased as a hard copy at www .luc-bodin.com/2012/12/06/livre-preparez-vous-au-changement/.

Bibliography

Anastasiou, Olga, and Jacqueline Mandelbaum. "Risque épigénétique et assistance médicale à la procreation." *Médecine de la Reproduction* 8, no. 3 (May–June 2006): 190–99.

Astier, Pierre. "Energie noire, la grande inconnue." *CNRS: Le Journal* 181 (February 2005).

Biet, Elodie. "Un polymorphisme protège les obèses de l'insulino-résistance." *Quotidien du Médecin* (March 20, 2008).

Blum, Jean. *Les Cathares, du Graal au secret de la mort joyeuse.* Monaco: Editions du Rocher, 1999.

Bogdanov, Igor, and Grichka Bogdanov. *Le visage de Dieu.* Paris: Grasset, 2010.

Braden, Gregg. *Fractal Time.* Carlsbad, Calif.: Hay House, 2013.

———. *The Spontaneous Healing of Belief.* Carlsbad, Calif.: Hay House, 2009.

Brecher, Paul. *Secrets of Energy Work.* London: Dorling Kindersley, 2001.

Byrne, Rhonda. *The Secret.* Hillsboro, Ore.: Atria/Beyond Words, 2006.

Cha, K. Y., D. P. Wirth, and R. A. Loba. "Does Prayer Influence the Success of In Vitro Fertilization-Embryo Transfer? Report of a Masked, Randomized Trial." *Journal of Reproductive Medicine* 46, no. 9 (2001): 781–87.

Chopra, Deepak. *Quantum Healing: Exploring the Frontiers of Mind Body Medicine.* New York: Bantam, 1990.

Clerc, Olivier. *The Gift of Forgiveness*. Forres, Scotland: Findhorn Press, 2010.

Dab, Dorianne. *Du Big Bang à la guérison*. Aubagne, France: Editions Quintessence, 2003.

Del Castillo, Paola. *La psychogénéalogie appliquée*. Aubagne, France: Quintessence, 2002.

Dericquebourg, Régis. *Religions de guérison*. Paris: Editions du Cerf, 1988.

Dossey, Larry. *Prayer Is Good Medicine*. New York: Harper, 1997.

Drouot, Patrick. *Nous sommes tous immortels*. Monaco: Editions du Rocher, 2005.

Dumas, Cécile. "Epigénétique: marqué à vie avant la naissance." *Sciences et Avenir* (October 28, 2008).

Dyer, Wayne. *The Power of Intention*. Carlsbad, Calif.: Hay House, 2004.

Emoto, Masaru. *The Hidden Messages in Water*. New York: Atria, 2005.

———. *The Miracle of Water*. New York: Atria, 2011.

Farrington, Alice. *Historical Atlas of Religions*. New York: Checkmark Books, 2002.

Ferrini, Paul. *L'amour sans conditions*. Quebec City, Canada: Le Dauphin Blanc, 2006.

Ford, Debbie. *Secret of the Shadow*. New York: Harper, 2002.

Fowler, J. H., and N. A. Christakis. "Dynamic Spread of Happiness in a Large Social Network: Longitudinal Analysis over 20 Years in the Framingham Heart Study." *British Medical Journal* 337, no. a2338 (2008): 1–9.

Gassette, Grace, and Georges Barbarin. *La clé: enseignement recueilli*. Paris: Astra, 1950.

Genel, Jean-Claude. *La voie parfait: le catharisme vivant*. N.p.: Editions des 3 Monts, 2006.

Genevès, Jean-François. *Le réferentiel de l'homme nouveau*. Self-published, 2000.

Griffe, Maurice. *Les Cathares: chronologie de 1022 à 1321*. Le Cannet, France: Éditions TSH, 2006.

Harris, W. S., M. Gouda, et al., "A Randomized Controlled Trial of the Effects of Remote, Intercessory Prayer on Outcomes in Patients Admitted to the Coronary Care Unit." *Archives of Internal Medicine* 159, no. 19 (October 25, 1999): 2273–78.

Hawking, Stephen. *The Universe in a Nutshell.* New York: Bantam, 2001.

Institut Curie and CNRS. "Epigénétique et cancer: Les liens se resserrent." *Centre National de la Recherche Scientifique et Institut Curie* (November 29, 2006). Available at http://curie.fr/sites/default/files/cancer-epigenetique-institut-curie.pdf.

Jampolsky, Gerald. *Teach Only Love.* New York: Atria, 2000.

Jung, Carl Gustav. *La Guérison psychologique.* Geneva: Georg, 1953.

———. *Seminar on Dream Analysis.* Princeton, N.J.: Princeton University Press, 1984.

Kerviel, Jean-Noël. *L'être humain et les énergies vibratoires.* Paris: Arka, 1997.

Kribbe, Pamela. *The Jeshua Channelings: Christ Consciousness in a New Era.* Bradenton, Fla.: Booklocker.com, 2008.

Lakhovsky, Georges. *L'origine de la vie: La radiation et les êtres vivants.* Paris: Éditions Nilsson, 1925.

Lao Tzu. *Tao Te Ching.*

Lassus, René de. *La communication efficace par la PNL.* Paris: Marabout, 2007.

Lebrun, Maguy. *Médicins du ciel, Médicins de la Terre.* Paris: Robert Laffont, 1987.

Londechamp, Guy. *L'homme vibratoire.* Plazac-Rouffignac, France: Amrita, 1998.

Morgan, Marlo. *Mutant Messenger Down Under.* New York: Harper, 2004.

Morse, Melvin. *La divine connexion.* Paris: Le Jardin des Livres, 2002.

Murphy, Joseph. *Techniques in Prayer Therapy.* San Gabriel, Calif.: Willing Pub., 1960.

Nexus (November–December 2004): 44–45.

Ornish, Dean, Mark Jesus M. Magbanua, Gerdi Weidner, et al.

"Changes in Prostate Gene Expression in Men Undergoing an Intensive Nutrition and Lifestyle Intervention." *Proceedings of the National Academy of Sciences* 105, no. 24, 8369–74.

Ortoli, Sven, and Jean-Pierre Pharabod. *La cantique des quantiques.* Paris: La Découverte/Poche, 2007.

Pahin, Jean-Yves. *Le Baptême d'esprit.* Plazac-Rouffignac, France: Amrita, 1993.

Pauwels, Louis, and Jacques Bergier. *Le matin des magiciens.* Paris: Gallimard, 1973.

———. English language edition: *The Morning of the Magicians.* Rochester, Vt.: Destiny, 2009.

Poletti, Rosette, and Barbara Dobbs. *L'estime de soi.* Saint-Julien-en-Genevois, France: Jouvence, 1998.

Portelance, Colette. *La guérison intérieur par l'acceptation et le lâcher-prise.* Saint-Julien-en-Genevois, France: Jouvence, 2009.

Quotimed.com. "Exposition in utero à la pollution." *Quotidien du Médicin* (February 15, 2009). Available at www.lequotidiendumedecin.fr/actualites/article/2009/02/15/lexposition-utero-la-pollution_237521.

Ransford, Emmanuel. "Un monde déconcertant: un pas dans la psycho-matière." Available at www.parasciences.net/spip.php?article187.

Redfield, James. *The Tenth Insight.* New York: Grand Central, 1998.

Reeves, Hubert. *L'Univers expliqué à mes petits-enfants.* Paris: Editions du Seuil, 2011.

Sauvageot, François. *Les yeux d'Uranie: Le regard et les mots des mathématiciens.* Available at http://educmath.ens-lyon.fr/Educmath/ressources/actes-en-ligne/canada-france-education/uranie.pdf.

Schaller, Christian Tal. *L'univers des chamanes: Le don de guérir est en chacun de nous.* Embourg, Belgium: Testez Éditions, 2006.

Schucman, Helen (scribe). *A Course in Miracles.* New York: The Foundation for Inner Peace, 2008.

Schützenberger, Ancelin. *Exercices pratiques de psychogénéalogie pour découvrir ses secrets de famille.* Paris: Payot et Rivages, 2011.

Schwitzgedel, V. M. "Role de l'épigénétique dans le diabète et la croissance." *Revue Médicale Suisse* (February 28, 2007).

Science & Vie. "La vie serait quantique: sens de l'odorat." *Science et Vie* 1123 (April 2011): 64–65.

Sciences et Avenir.com (J. I.). "Variabilité génétique." *Sciences et Avenir* (June 27, 2008). Available at www.sciencesetavenir.fr/fondamental/20080627.OBS0384/variabilite-genetique.html.

Sellam, Salomon. *Le Syndrome du Gisant: un subtil enfant de remplacement.* Saint André de Sangonis, France: Berangel, 2004.

Simonton, Carl. *Getting Well Again: The Bestselling Classic About the Simontons' Revolutionary Lifesaving Self-Awareness Techniques.* New York: Bantam, 1992.

———. *The Healing Journey: The Simonton Center Program for Achieving Physical, Mental, and Spiritual Health.* New York: Bantam, 1992.

Smith, Cyril W., and Simon Best. *Electromagnetic Man: Health and Hazard in the Electrical Environment.* New York: Saint Martins, 1989.

Tipping, Colin C. *Radical Forgiveness: Making Room for the Miracle.* Marietta, Ga.: Global 13 Publications, 2001.

Valois, Brigitte. "Le rôle des phénomènes épigénétiques." *Quotidien du Médicin* (June 16, 2008).

Vitale, Joe, and Ihaleakala Hew Len. *Zero Limits.* New York: Wiley, 2007.

Weiss, Brian. *Many Lives, Many Masters: The True Story of a Prominent Psychiatrist, His Young Patient, and the Past-Life Therapy that Changed Both Their Lives.* New York: Simon and Schuster/Fireside, 1988.

About the Authors

Luc Bodin

Luc Bodin is a medical doctor specializing in holistic medicine with a degree in clinical cancer treatment. He is also scientific adviser for several health magazines and the author of numerous books in the health field that look at energy healing and illnesses such as cancer, Alzheimer's disease, and fibromyalgia.

He also presents workshops and training on energy treatments in France, Belgium, Switzerland, Canada, and French Polynesia, which are open to all.

His website is **www.luc-bodin.us**.

Nathalie Bodin Lamboy

Nathalie Bodin Lamboy is a public speaker and author in the field of personal development. She has written six books, translated into five languages, on Ho'oponopono. She is also a feng shui expert who has received training in energetic and psycho-energetic disciplines.

Her website is **www.livinghooponopono.com**.

Jean Graciet

Jean Graciet is a practitioner of NLP and Ericksonian hypnosis, and specializes in the study of the meaning of symptoms and diseases. He offers lectures and workshops on the themes of relationships, individual evolution, and the awakening of consciousness. Since 2010, in the company of his wife, Maria-Elisa Graciet-Hurtado, he has primarily devoted his time to spreading the message of "Ho'oponopono, a path to consciousness," through conferences, workshops, audio CDs, and a card deck.

Their websites are **www.eveiletsante.fr** and **www.mercijetaime.fr**.

Index